ELVIS PRESLEY

Elvis on stage in Las Vegas:

'My ex-wife is right there. Stand up Priscilla, and let them see you! She's beautiful – I knows 'em when I picks 'em. Hold little Lisa up too. We have a fantastic relationship. We are the best of friends and always have been. Our divorce came about, not because of another man, or because of another woman, but because of the circumstances involving my career. And nothing else! Regardless of what you have read, or have been lead to believe. I didn't think it was fair on Priscilla . . .'

D1638691

ELVIS PRESLEY

Todd Slaughter

A MANDABROOK BOOK

First published in Great Britain by
Mandabrook Ltd, 1977
Reprinted 1977 (twice)

Copyright © Mandabrook Ltd, 1977

ISBN: 0 427 00417 9

Printed in Great Britain by
Richard Clay (The Chaucer Press), Ltd, Bungay, Suffolk

To my world – Ada, John,
Vikki and Gregory

CHAPTER ONE

On October 9th, 1973 Elvis Presley and his wife Priscilla (nee Beaulieu) drove to the Santa Monica Court House. They were there to endorse their signatures to a document. An act which minutes later would set in action the news agency tele-printer keys throughout the world, tapping out the story of Elvis Presley's divorce.

On October 9th, 1973 Elvis Presley became a human being for the first time since 1956 when his first major single record 'Heartbreak Hotel' blockbusted its way to the top of every Western hit parade. Elvis Presley – even the name is unique!

On October 9th, 1973 Elvis Presley was a human being again, not simply because his divorce proceedings were now finalised, but because Elvis had actually gone through the motions of getting divorced. With this one act Elvis had smashed the shackles which had previously set him apart from the rest of the human race. With this one act, Elvis proved to the world that he too was human. He too could find difficulty in making his marriage work, because Elvis wasn't perfect.

Elvis was heartbroken. Tragedy had now manifested itself twice in his life – the death of his mother and the loss of his wife. Throughout his career we, his fans, had 'canonised' Elvis to the point of absurdity. All followers had disassociated themselves from the raw obscene Presley of the mid-fifties. Most had preferred to forget the gipsy-like extrovert who as legend has it teased his female audiences at early concerts. As often as Elvis had tried to escape from his all-perfect image, his disciples imprisoned him more securely with immediate denials of anything slightly untoward. The media too, anxious not to offend his followers, co-operated. Besides they had 'spending power', and no-one offends a man and his money, though all try to separate him from it.

When Elvis was called to serve his country in compulsory military service, he enlisted in the US Army. He didn't evade his duty, though many of his contemporaries tried. The Draft Board Commissioners did delay his induction, because a movie was to be completed. Elvis could have opted for the Forces Entertainment Corps, but anxious to do his bit, he was shipped to Germany ... hundreds of miles away from any possible action. Besides, Elvis was to become the biggest recruitment drive aid the US Government had ever experienced.

During his absence Elvis was never forgotten, and by the time he was brought back to civilian life his public requested more of the clean-cut Presley we had all grown to love. His mentor, Colonel Parker obliged, and Elvis continued to entertain to our demands. Elvis had become the gentleman, the country squire of rock 'n' roll. When Elvis was married to Priscilla, it was as if he was partnering a look-a-like. Press photographs showed them as 'brother and sister'. Priscilla was beautiful, and Elvis was handsome. But Priscilla was not more beautiful than Elvis was handsome. They were the perfect match – make up artistes had seen to that. Happily, nine months later Priscilla gave birth to Lisa Marie Presley. We were all overjoyed, and in the minds of Elvis' fans it was an immaculate conception. Why, it had to be! Elvis wouldn't do anything like that – of course it was a virgin birth.

On October 9th, 1973 Elvis Presley and his wife Priscilla were divorced. We had all heard rumours of a separation a year before, but it couldn't be true – could it? Priscilla was known to have had an association with an Hawaiian karate champion, but surely this was for extra tuition, in spite of the press reports to the contrary. In his defence fans echoed reports of a two million dollar settlement, and lawyers' comments at the time emphasised how willing Elvis had been to ensure such a generous award to his ex-wife, and continued monetary security for daughter Lisa Marie. But that was all we could do to heal the wound, and of course it didn't – Elvis' marriage had ended.

But what now for Elvis? His marriage to Priscilla had precipitated his return to live appearances following six years of isolation inside the safety of the movie studios. Would

Elvis' career continue to develop, or stagnate? Most feel it has stagnated since his separation.

The split in 1972, followed by the decree nisi a year later gave the media room for manoeuvre. On the whole the gossip magazines had left Elvis and Priscilla alone during wedlock, but now it was as if they had received carte blanche from Elvis himself to drag the sewers for any story. Their effect upon Elvis was traumatic. Elvis was hit right between the eyes with reports that offended his public and his inner self. Elvis needed the media's protection at a time when he was to be found naked of support from all sides. Not that the fans were letting Elvis down, but we were confused. In an effort to dispel some of his self inflicted guilt, Elvis would halt his stage presentations to deliver his comments upon the situation, and to attack those who had hurt him.

'I don't read movie mags. That stuff is junk! If they [the journalists] don't know something about me, they make it up. I know they have a job to do – they have to write something – but if I had done one tenth of what they say, my karate instructor would not allow me to wear that belt. I would not be who I am – I would not walk out on this stage. I could not face my daughter, or my father.'

As if desperate to get his side across, Elvis would often falter with emotion, and consequently fail to give as good as he was getting from the media. Elvis used every excuse during his 1974 Las Vegas season to halt his show – to present his case. 'I would like to introduce you to a friend of mine [seated in the audience]. He was head of the Narcotics Division in Los Angeles for 26 years. His name is John O'Grady, and he has a book coming out called *O'Grady*.' At this point Elvis showed the volume to the multitude, holding the work in his right hand as if he was about to take an oath. 'There's three chapters about the recent paternity suit filed against me. He [O'Grady] handled it, and it turned out to be a complete conspiracy and hoax. I had my picture taken with this chick – that's all. John is now a private investigator and he's a good friend of mine. You talk about *Superfly*, you talk about *Batman and Robin*, you talk about the *French Connection* – this guy makes 'em all look like Mickey Mouse!

'I was sick one day last week. I had a temperature of 102°. I had the 'flu and missed two shows. I can't get sick – they say I am "strung out". From three different sources I heard that I was strung out on heroin. I've never been strung out in my life. They don't give you a black belt if you're strung out. These reports are damaging to my little daughter, to Priscilla, to my father, my doctor, my friends, everyone on stage, and YOU!' Elvis then showed his audience a certificate. 'This is from the International Narcotics Enforcement Association. This awards special honours and life memebership of the Association – to ME! I have carried a Federal Narcotics Association badge for six years – they don't give you one of these if you're strung out.'

Elvis' outbursts were unusual, and most out of character. We never knew how distressed Elvis was, yet we were all in sympathy with his grief. In 1974 Priscilla too came in for attack, following misinterpretations connected with some of the things Elvis had reported from the stage. To remedy any possible misconstruction he would frequently tongue-tie himself into further ambiguity. However, once he got it about right, after a more than usual dramatic rendition of 'Lord, You Gave Me A Mountain'. Elvis added, 'I would like to make something clear with regard to that particular song. It talks about a wife, and the taking of a baby, and so forth; and somewhere along the line it's being associated with me. It's a beautiful song, and was written by Marty Robbins. [Elvis points to the audience.] My ex-wife is right there. Stand up Priscilla, and let them see you! She's beautiful – I knows 'em when I picks 'em. Hold little Lisa up too. We have a fantastic relationship. We are the best of friends and always have been. Our divorce came about, not because of another man, or because of another woman, but because of the circumstances involving my career. And nothing else! Regardless of what you have read, or have been lead to believe. I didn't think it was fair on Priscilla, with me being gone so often, and travelling so much. So therefore, as decently as you can do such a thing, we just made an agreement to always be close and care, because we have a daughter to raise, and for her [Priscilla] to have whatever she wanted as a settlement. After the settlement –

two million or whatever – I gave my ex-wife a mink coat, worth $15,000, and bought her a Jag! That's the kind of relationship we have! She ordered me a $42,000 white Rolls Royce. That's not a bad set-up is it? – I'm getting a little back! I'm not hurting so bad, and I got a little of it back! She bought the car by herself as a gesture of love!'

Proud father, proud son, proud ex-husband, and surrounded by the trivia of beautiful women again. But were we left with only half the Elvis we all started out with back in the farmlands of the Mississippi, some forty or more years ago?

In 1969 Elvis told his 'life story' to the two thousand members of the audience in Las Vegas during one of his first live appearance seasons in the International Hotel. 'I'd like to tell you a little bit about how I got started in the business. A lot has been written about it, but never from my side. A good deal has been inaccurate, and a lot of the writers don't know the real story. I had just left high school, and whilst I was studying to be an electrician, I was driving a truck. And I got wired the wrong way! One day in 1954 I was driving my truck and during my lunch break I went into a little record shop, and I made a record for a guy. A little demonstration record. It was played on the radio in Memphis – Memphis – Memphis, that's my home town [you have to be loose when you say it]. "Where're you from boy?" If I get any looser, I might just fall apart. Anyhow, this guy put out the record and it sold pretty well in my home town. Then I started appearing in little clubs, in and around Memphis – Memphis – Memphis, and in those days you never saw anyone with side burns and long hair. People used to say, "Who's he?" – "He just out of the trees man!" Singers never moved much on stage in those days.

'Nobody really knew who I was until I met this Colonel Sanders – no, I mean Colonel Parker. I was working for about a year and a half in night clubs, in football fields, in bars and on the "Louisiana Hayride", and then I met Colonel Parker. They put me on TV. In 1956 I did shows for Jackie Gleason, Milton Berle, Ed Sullivan, and Steve Allen. They dressed me in a tuxedo on the Steve Allen show, and filmed me waist up. I had to stand perfectly still. I couldn't move. They had me singing to a dog. Imagine – here I am singing "You ain't nothin' but a Hound Dog ..." and there's this dog looking at me. Then the dog starts jumping about – so they had to take it away! So they filmed me from the waist up – it was pretty hairy back then.

'I got to Hollywood too, though I wasn't ready for it. And Hollywood wasn't ready for me. I made "Love Me Tender", "Loving You", loving her, loving anything I could get my hands on at the time. Then came "Jailhouse Rock", and now I'm getting used to the life. I'm a movie star, I'm a movie star – eating hamburgers, and drinking Pepsi! Then I made "King Creole", and then I went into the Army – I got drafted and went into the army for 2 years. The guys were watching me to see what I would do. When they saw I was doing everything, just as they were – everything was alright. But it wasn't easy. In 1960 I got out and returned to Hollywood. I made "GI Blues", "Girls, Girls, Girls", and several pictures that did very well for me. But as the years passed by, I really missed the people. Audience contact – I was really getting the bug! I was doing so many movies, I couldn't really do what I wanted. They'd say "Action!", and I'd say "Huh, Huh, Huh, Memphis – Memphis – Memphis". And they would say, "That ain't what you're supposed to say," and I'd reply "Huh?"

'Well, that's why I'm here tonight. So if you think that long hair and side-burns are freaky now – 14 years ago I couldn't walk down the street in Memphis – Memphis – Memphis.'

CHAPTER TWO

'From the time I was very young, I knew something was going to happen to me. I didn't know exactly what, but it was feeling that the future looked kinda bright.'

Once upon a time there was a girl named Gladys Smith, and a boy called Vernon Presley. They lived in a Mississippi newtown called Tupelo – the name derived from the Chickasaw word meaning 'Lodging Place'. Gladys was a sewing machine operator and Vernon worked, when he could, on the land. Times were hard and the local economy left much to be desired. Vernon and Gladys met and, within a matter of weeks, they were married in a town not far from their home. They made a handsome couple! He was blond – she was dark. He was 17 – she was 21. (Vernon had a brother called Vester. Gladys had a sister called Cletis. A few years later they married, and Vester now works on Elvis' Memphis estate.)

In the summer of 1934 Gladys learned that she was pregnant, so she was forced to quite her job in the rag trade. Vernon however had moved off the land and was delivering milk from door to door – a practice still common in Britain, but virtually extinct in the United States. The Presleys needed a house, and a loan was arranged from Vernon's employer. They awaited the birth with excitement, although both were already well below the poverty line.

In the afternoon of January 8th, 1935 Elvis Aron Presley was born, one of identical twins. The second son, christened Jesse Garon, was still-born. The dead baby was buried the following day in an unmarked grave, and Mr and Mrs Presley concentrated all their love on the baby Elvis.

Elvis grew up amongst friendly people, brought about by the tightness of the community. Religion was the order of the day, yet no-one considered themselves fanatical towards God.

11

It was what they knew, and all had grown up into this way of life. 'My mama would never let me out of her sight. I couldn't go down to the creek with other kids.'

Families would congregate once each month for outdoor meetings. These gatherings could be described as 'Holy Picnics', and as well as fun and entertainment for the children, there was teaching in the ways of the Lord from visiting Ministers. Like all meetings they concluded with singing in the evening around a camp fire. 'We used to go to these religious sing-ins all the time. The preachers used to cut-up all over the place – that's how I was introduced to the on-stage wiggle. The preachers did it! And the congregation loved it – why I even remember one day a preacher jumping on to a piano. I never did that!'

Elvis was surrounded by music, and most of it was derived through the church. 'I first realised I could sing when I was two years old. In Church I would love to hear the choir. My mother told me that when I was two years old I would slide off her lap and stand there singing. I could carry a tune, even though I didn't know the words. Maybe I wasn't always in tune, but you could sure hear me above the rest.

'When I was four or five all I looked forward to was Sundays, when we would all go to Church. I loved the old church, filled with sunlight, and the security of my mother and father beside me. This was the only singing training I had – I never had lessons. I'd just try to sing as loud and in tune as I could. Later mama and daddy and I would all sing together at revival meetings. I was always singing. People living on the same housing project as me would stop and listen.'

At the age of 5, blond haired Elvis was enrolled for school, yet his singing ability wasn't noticed until a change in teachers brought forth a kindly scholastic called Mrs Grimes. It was this lady who remembered Elvis singing 'Old Shep' during morning prayers in the school chapel, and she asked the school headmaster to let Elvis sing the song for him. 'I was about eight years old. They liked the song and they entered me in a local talent competition. I even won a prize.' The talent show was an annual one staged as part of the festivities of the Mississippi–Alabama State Fair. Elvis sang his 'Old Shep', unaccompanied, without microphone, standing on a chair. He won second prize – five dollars, and free admission on all the fair's amusements.

Northern Mississippi was cruel to the poor folks of the time. War was being waged in Europe, and the United States was gradually feeling the effect. The weather too brought disaster to farmers who relied on the success of their annual crops. This disaster was then passed on to the farm workers who relied on the land as their only form of income. Vernon Presley was by now back on the land, but the family was getting poorer. Vernon and Gladys made sure that young Elvis wasn't deprived of anything even if his wishes meant them going without real food. There was one request though they had to refuse. Elvis wanted a bike, but they persuaded him to accept a guitar as a substitute. 'I really wanted that bicycle, but daddy couldn't afford one. So he bought me a guitar for around twelve bucks. I know even this was a great sacrifice – he went without smokes for several weeks. I learned to play by listening to the radio, and other people's phonograph records. Uncle Johnny and Uncle Vester tried to help me too, but they could only show me a few chords. I guess I learnt most of it from the radio station in Tupelo. I used to listen quite a lot, and I loved records by Sister Rosetta Thorpe and country singers like Roy Acuff, Ernest Tubbs, Ted Daffan, Jimmie Rodgers, Jimmy Davis, and Bob Wills.'

Elvis also began listening to black singers. Blues singers from the same neighbourhood began to influence the young Presley, especially John Lee Hooker, BB King, and Howlin' Wolf, and on Wednesdays Elvis would attend the revival meetings at the First Assembly of God Church to learn the singing styles of the ethnic spirituals.

Vernon Presley was now dependent on social security, and there was no alternative but to move away from the depressed Tupelo homesteads. Elvis was 13 years old and it was now 1948, three years after the war. 'We were broke, man, real broke. Dad packed all our belongings into boxes and put them into our 1939 Plymouth. We left Tupelo overnight, and headed for Memphis. Things just had to get better.'

But of course the streets of Memphis weren't paved with

gold either and the Presleys had it rough for many months. Their first dwelling was a room on Poplar Avenue – downtown Memphis – and though very cramped, it was home. Gladys Presley took care of Elvis' education and arranged for him to have a place in L.C. Humes High School. The education establishment was old, and enormous in comparison to what the Tupelo boy had been used too. There were almost 1,700 pupils making up its six classes. Throughout, Elvis kept himself to himself, mixing with others only in sporting activities, and with those who used to appreciate his guitar picking and singing. Everyone noticed the close bond between Elvis and his mother. 'When we moved to Memphis and I started high school, my mama still walked me to school. In fact she escorted me even when I was 15. Daddy mostly drove trucks, and when he used to bring them home, I used to sit in them. He never made much money but anything I wanted, he would try and get for me.'

In fact Vernon's first job in Memphis was in the employ of the United Paint Company as a packer. The pay was regular, and overtime brought his income up to almost $40 a week. The Poplar Avenue property was not in good order, and in the summer of 1949 the family were moved to a new community housing project known as Lauderdale Courts, in Winchester Street. The accommodation, a two bedroomed ground floor apartment, was subsidised by the civic authorities with a rent established in accordance with each tenant's individual needs. The Presley's paid $35 each month.

Unlike all the other boys in his class, Elvis grew his hair long and with early maturity he was able to cultivate very respectable side-burns. His taste for clothes was also extrovert. One day he'd be seen in a pink coat and black strides – the following day pink trousers and a black jacket. Elvis bought his clothing from a store which generally supplied stage wear for the country and western acts of the area. Elvis used this stage apparel for daytime dress, and to draw attention to himself. Elvis was in the throes of establishing his own identity, though to what end he didn't know at the time. Lansky Brothers, the clothing store on Second Street helped him. 'I liked clothes. When the folks at Lansky's told me I

14

could buy clothes on hire-purchase, I told 'em – I don't trade like that! When I have me some money, I'm gonna come in and buy you out.' A promise he kept a couple of years later.

Elvis remained reluctant to perform before anyone he didn't class as a friend. He would go out of his way to avoid public confrontation between himself, his guitar, and an unknown audience. However, Miss Scrivener, his history teacher, had heard tales of the young Presley's talents and subsequently enlisted his services for the school concert. Elvis was not at all pleased, and he was reported to have been quite screwed up every time he thought about it. 'In my 11th grade they entered me into another show. I thought nobody knew that I sang. I was very shy, and I didn't consider myself popular at school. I wasn't even dating anyone. Anyway, I came out and performed "Cold Cold Icy Fingers". When a student did well, he was invited to do an encore. Mildred Scrivener said, "They like you, go out there and do another song!"

'So I did. I sang "Till I Waltz with You Again", and I heard a loud rumbling – it must have been applause. After the act I said "They really did like me, didn't they Miss Scrivener?" I was amazed how popular I was at school after that concert.' The only other recorded time it was known that Elvis performed publically in those days was during a visit to the Memphis Veterans Hospital, when he sang and played with the members of the Odd Fellows Boys Club.

In November 1950 Elvis took a job at a local cinema. 'Until I came to Memphis I had never been to the movies. I liked them a lot. I got a job at Loews State theatre which made me about 14 bucks. I was strong, and so I was able to work hard. I also mowed lawns.'

Feeling the benefit of cash in his pockets Elvis quit his five hours a night stint at the movie palace, and worked a full night shift at the Marl Metal Products Company. It didn't really work though – Elvis would fall asleep during class. 'We all worked hard. When my father hurt his back, my mother worked in the wards of St Joseph's Hospital. She bathed patients, she made beds, scrubbed floors, and worked harder than ever before. In the evening she would come home and cook supper, do housework, and mend other people's clothes.'

15

In the Summer of '53 Elvis left school. He worked initially for the Precision Tool Company, but he didn't like it. 'So I drove a truck for Crown Electric which paid $35 a week, and in the evenings I studied electricity.' Crown was an electrical subcontracting firm situated on Poplar Avenue, and he would practise his singing on everyone he came across, especially the people working for Crown. 'I used to go down to the fire station, and sing to the boys there. They were the only ones around Memphis who seemed to have a lot of listening time.'

Every day, on his delivery rounds Elvis would pass the Memphis Recording Service Office, a division of Sam Phillips' Sun Recording Company. One lunch hour he parked his truck, and took $4 to the assistant in the reception. 'It was my mother's birthday, and I had decided to make her a record. I went to Sun, paid my four bucks to the lady, because I had a notion to find out what I really sounded like. I had been singing all my life and I was kinda curious. But when I heard the record it was terrible. I was terrible. I sounded like someone banging a trash can lid. I figured Mom would like it anyway. In fact, she borrowed a record player from a neighbour, and played it over and over 'til it was plumb near wore out.'

During this recording, engineer, receptionist, secretary Marion Keisker, decided to listen in. Half way through the first cut 'My Happiness' she was tempted to switch on the standby tape recorder, and though she missed most of it, she was able to record all of the second song, 'That's When Your Heartaches Begin'. It was her intentions to replay the tape to label boss Sam Phillips, as she'd always remembered him saying, 'If you could find a white man, with a negro's voice we could make a billion.'

When he heard the song, Sam was impressed, though he said that there was still a lot of work for the youth to do. Ensuring that Marion had Elvis' name and address on record he went about his business. In fact several months passed by and Elvis visited the studios again. This time Sam was in on his own. He told Elvis that Miss Keisker was impressed with his voice, and so too was Phillips when Elvis cut two more tracks, 'Casual Love' and 'I'll Never Stand in Your Way'. More months passed, and despite Miss Keisker's continual barracking for Phillips to record Elvis Presley, he'd always reply by saying that he was not yet ready, or the right song wasn't available.

Meanwhile the Presley family went about their day to day routines. Vernon Presley continued to pack cans of paint, and Elvis was still delivery boy at Crown. Elvis would often tune his radio to WMPS, and go out of his way to watch live broadcasts of country artistes. Bob Neal was the DJ who hosted the top country show 'High Noon Roundup', and it was the same Neal who was eventually to become Elvis' personal manager for a time. Elvis was also drawn to late night gospel sessions, and the music of the forbidden black ghettos.

Finally Sam Phillips found a song which he thought suitable for Presley. Marion hurriedly found his file, and after several attempts reached Elvis by phone. 'It was 12 o'clock on a Saturday, and they said "Can you be there by three?" I ran all the way. I was there by the time they had hung up the phone. I guess I must have sung for three hours.' The song selected for Elvis was 'Without You'. 'I sang everything I knew – pop, ballads, spirituals, just for a warm up.' Meanwhile Sam called guitarist Scotty Moore, and arranged for Elvis to see him later that evening. Scotty and Elvis talked, and sang a few songs together. Bassist Bill Black, hearing the noise, popped in, and popped out just as quickly. After Elvis had left, Scotty Moore told Phillips that he wasn't really impressed. But a studio session was arranged for Monday, as a trial, and a small group of session men, headed by Scotty Moore hammered out a few songs. It wasn't impressive: in fact everyone, except Elvis, was disappointed. However, months of intensive rehearsals followed, until Sam finally said, 'OK boys, this is the session.'

The first song recorded was 'I Love You Because', followed by 'That's Alright Mama'. 'We cut these and "Blue Moon of Kentucky", I think. I sang them with a rock-a-billy beat, which was unusual as they were really black blues songs.' Sam was elated. He took the demonstration disc to a DJ called Dewey Phillips (no known relation of Sam) who hosted a radio show called 'Red Hot and Blue' on station WHBQ. At home Mrs Presley tuned in her radio, and Elvis vanished – into hiding in the stalls of a local movie theatre. 'On the night I went to

17

see a movie. I was too nervous to sit with Mom to hear the transmission. However my parents came looking for me because the radio station received lots of calls.'

Sun Records were totally unprepared. They were flooded with orders for the disc before they had even 'mastered' the songs. From now on Elvis was to perform the local club circuit with Scotty and Bill Black who split their own band, the 'Starlight Wranglers'. By July '54 'That's Alright Mama' was number 3 in the local Memphis hit parade. 'The disc sold over 7,000 in Memphis, and almost 20,000 in total. Mom was so excited and happy, but dad wasn't so sure. He used to say he knew a lot of people who played the guitar, and didn't work. "Just make up your mind if you want to be an electrician or play a guitar. I never knew a guitar player worth a damn!"'

CHAPTER THREE

'The very first appearance I made after I started recording was on the bill of a show in Memphis – a
big charity jamboree in an outdoor auditorium, the
Shell in Overton Park, Memphis. I was an extra
added attraction. I was on stage, and doing a fast
number, and everyone began screaming and hollering. I said "What did I do, What did I do?" I came
off stage and the manager told me that everyone was
hollering, because I was wiggling. He said "Go back
on to the stage and do it some more." So I did,
eleven times. I didn't realise that my body was
moving – it's a natural thing to me!"

It must have been quite convincing at the time such an inter-
view was first reported, though no-one now doubts that Elvis
was so oblivious to his built in sexual sales aides. Elvis
Presley was never that naïve!

Marion Keisker, and for that matter, everyone at Sun
Records, had gone to town promoting the first Presley single.
Over 1,000 promotional copies were mailed to radio station
personnel, but they were all conscious that the majority were
never given air-time. The black stations wouldn't play it because the artiste was white. The white stations ignored it because it sounded too black. Others said it was too country to be
played after 5.00 am. However, enough stations supported the
release to enable it to maintain it's high local position. Success
in sales opened doors into live radio. The two leading country shows of the area were Nashville's WSM production
'Grand Old Opry', and Shreveport's 'Louisiana Hayride', and
Elvis performed for both.

Elvis appeared on the Opry stage with Scotty and Bill, but
his act was not well received. It was said that Elvis' lack of
success on this occasion almost destroyed him, and that he

19

sobbed all the way back to Memphis. As Elvis left the stage, link man Jim Denny suggested that he should go back to driving a truck. A comment which Elvis never forgot. In fact when Denny put his arm round Presley some years later during a trade reception and commented 'I always knew this guy would make it', Elvis was heard to mutter in reply 'The son of a bitch doesn't remember the time when he broke my heart!'

However his KWKH–Shreveport appearance was much more successful. 'I went down to the *Louisiana Hayride*, as just a try out, more or less. I went down once, and returned a couple of weeks later. And the people seemed to like me, they kinda went for the songs I did. So they gave me a job down there.' In fact the show's programme director, Horace Logan was so taken aback that he gave Elvis a contract for 12 months. This season of broadcasting was just the break Elvis had hoped for. On his first show Elvis stammered through his introduction, 'I-I-I'd like t'say how happy we are to be out here. It's a great honour for us to get a chance to appear on the *Louisiana Hayride*. We're gonna do a song that we've got on Sun.' Halfway through the series however, Presley was becoming the seasoned broadcaster ripping into commercials along the lines of 'You can get 'em piping hot after 4 pm. You can get 'em piping hot – Southern Made Doughnuts. Hits on the Spot!'

Elvis was now earning enough to quit his daytime job with Crown and concentrate on his act. DJ Fontana had now joined the band, and Elvis was being billed all over the Southern States as 'The Hillbilly Cat'. Elvis' appearance at that time on the bill at the Overton Park Shell in Memphis had its fair share of headaches. At one time it was ruled that he couldn't go on stage because he had yet to be accepted into the Musicians' Union. Reluctantly, the Union was forced to accept his fee.

Up to this time the band and Elvis were being handled by Scotty Moore, who acted as manager, plugger, booker, and general factotum. But it was becoming more and more obvious that a professional approach was required, now that Elvis' act and records were being reviewed in the nationwide trade papers. In 'Billboard' he ranked high in a DJ poll of 'most promising newcomers' in the Country Music field. The Memphis DJ, Bob Neal, already aware of the boy's potential opened negotiations with Elvis during the Overton Park show. As well as a DJ working on WMPS, Neal was a promoter and had had considerable experience, especially in the Country Music market. By the time Elvis' second Sun single was released (January 1955) Bob was holding the reins. 'Good Rockin' Tonight' backed with 'I Don't Care if the Sun Don't Shine' sold reasonably well in Memphis, reaching number 3 in the local chart, but didn't show itself in any other town.

Sun single number three was cut, pressed, and released. It again was another now-legendary track, 'Milkcow Blues Boogie', but at the time no-one thought it interesting enough to buy in sufficient quantities. But it was Elvis' third release, he had by now been issued with his first paternity suit, and fans were actively constructing a fan club.

In an attempt to broaden Presley's appeal, Bob Neal managed to include the 'Hillbilly Cat' act on 'The Hank Snow Jamboree'. This country and western package used Snow as top of the bill, and also included Slim Whitman, and Faron Young. The show toured all the South Eastern States, commencing in New Orleans on May 1st. It was promoted by Hank Snow's personal manager Colonel Tom Parker. Elvis' fourth Sun release was issued during the tour, and it could be said that Elvis' appearance in some six different States did nothing but help the sales of this new product, 'Baby, Lets Play House' coupled with 'I'm Left, You're Right, She's Gone!' In July this single became the first Elvis record to appear in the National Charts.

Colonel Parker, who had started out as a fair-ground barker cum showbusiness entrepreneur, had entered the Country Music circus as manager for Eddy Arnold in the forties. He had been aware of the existence of Elvis Presley for over a year and his recent dealings with Bob Neal brought him nearer to finally taking over the singer's personal management. Parker had always maintained that Elvis would always be a local star if he remained with Sun Records, and by the time Elvis' fifth Sun single was working its way up the charts the Colonel had activated a full frontal assault. Firstly he manoeuvred the

Presley parents into agreeing that he was the right manager for their son, and secondly he started to woo the larger record magnates.

Knowing full well that Elvis would be receiving notable accolades towards the end of the year with high category positions in a national trade publication's annual personality awards poll, the Colonel had decided that this was the right time to announce a change. Ahmet Ertegun, the president of Atlantic Records, offered $25,000 for the Presley contract, but negotiations with Steve Sholes, an old 'friend' of Colonel Parker, and an A & R man from RCA, proved more fruitful. Sam Phillips received $35,000 from RCA for his Presley–Sun contract which included all the previously released and unreleased material; and there was a bonus for Elvis of $5,000 as part of the deal.

All this meant that during the last few weeks of 1955 RCA had re-issued the previous five Sun Singles, and as Sun still had a sell-off period, both companies were involved in promoting the same product. A unique position for any artiste to enjoy.

Elvis' comments on the situation were as follows: 'It all happened so quickly. I got a call from Colonel Parker. He signed me, along with Scotty and Bill, and we just drove from town to town, wherever the Colonel got us bookings. Then the Colonel arranged for Steve Sholes of RCA to hear my records. He liked them, and they paid $35,000 to buy my contract from Sun. It was a lot of money. I had $5,000 too – I went out and bought Mama a pink Cadillac.' Elvis returned home for Christmas.

CHAPTER FOUR

1956

'I like my success and am very grateful, but I now appreciate what it is to walk on the street and go where you want without being stopped. Some of them tear at your clothing, and there's always the guy who makes insulting remarks, looking for a fight.'

On January 10th, two days after his 21st birthday Elvis went to the RCA Studios in Nashville, to cut his first product for the company. For Elvis it must have been like appearing inside a gold-fish bowl with the world looking in. And as far as Elvis was concerned this extra studio audience was to be his new world. Steve Sholes from RCA was in the control room, fingers crossed hoping that his investment was worthwhile. Colonel Parker was there keeping his eyes on his investment, and upon everyone else; and just in case he should miss anything, Tom Diskin – the Colonel's assistant – was there carrying out a secondary surveillance. In the studio with Elvis were musicians Scotty Moore, Bill Black, and DJ Fontana, plus session guitarist Chet Atkins. The local top vocal gospel group, the Jordanaires, were on hand to put in the 'Ooohs and Ahrrrs'. 'I Got a Woman', 'Money Honey', and 'Heartbreak Hotel', were recorded. The following day two more songs were canned – 'I'm Counting on You' and 'I was the One'. The latter song utilised the Jordanaires to the full, though they were reported to be unimpressed with RCA's new find. However Elvis liked the Jords. 'If any of these songs go big, I would be pleased if you guys would record all my stuff with me!'

Colonel Parker, ever conscious of the fact that records only sell if exposed, had concluded a deal with Tommy & Jimmy Dorsey for a series of appearances on their weekly half hour

CBS networked television show. On a wet January 28th, Elvis and his cronies ventured to New York, and in an undisciplined style Elvis introduced the nation to 'Heartbreak Hotel'. His body twisted and jerked, his movements were suggestive, and here he was, at last laying it on a hitherto conservative audience. Mail poured into the station and as was soon to be the norm, phone lines were jammed at CBS. Teenage America was beginning to adore their new idol, but the establishment was horrified. Elvis' reported replies to newspaper reports give the reader some idea as to the gravity of their affront. 'I don't do no dirty movements. I don't rightly know what "pornographic" means, and I never did a bump or grind in my life! I have to jump around when I sing – it ain't vulgar! It's just the way I feel – I can't even sing with a beat if I stand still. Any little movement I make seems to mean so much to my fans. I might close my eyes a minute, or put my hand up against my forehead – and they scream. It seems so natural. Those who are saying that I'm trying to be sexy have got it all wrong.' But had they? Was the coy-sounding Elvis, ever knowledgeable of his turn-on ability, getting frightened of what he had created?

'I put my whole heart into what I do – maybe people can see that! If I thought I was a bad influence, I'd give up singing, and go back to driving a truck. More than anything else, I want the folks back home to think right of me!' But as always, mama knows best: 'My mother told me, "Oh you're not vulgar, but you're putting too much into your singing." She also said that if I keep it up, I'll be dead by the time I'm 30!'

The pace built up, the RCA single rose to top the American hit parades. And now the strain was beginning to tell on Elvis. Following the last Dorsey show in March, Elvis and the boys left New York and drove to Los Angeles. After a show at the Coliseum they continued to San Diego, Southern California to appear with TV personality Milton Berle. Immediately afterwards they travelled to Denver, and by the time they reached Florida Elvis collapsed and was taken to Jacksonville Hospital. 'I was over-exhausted, and got too hot. I had hot flushes, and got dizzy. The doctor warned me if I didn't slow down a little,

I might have to lay off for two years. He said that I must do more work in the twenty or so minutes I'm on stage, than a labourer does in an eight-hour day.' Elvis got dressed the following morning, walked out of the hospital, and resumed his tour.

Elvis was circumnavigating the American states on an almost daily timetable, and near miss accidents were common-place. 'I was in a two-engine charter plane on the way to Nashville with Scotty, Bill, and DJ. Suddenly one of the engines failed. I was petrified, and all I could think to do was to pray. We had to remove sharp objects from our pockets, and rest our heads on pillows between our knees. Luckily, we found a deserted air-strip near at hand. I'm scared-stiff of flying now!' Fans too were becoming more dangerous than an everyday occupational hazard.

'I've never been seriously hurt. I've had my hair pulled and got a few scratches. I've lost a few suits of clothes too. As far as I'm concerned, if they want my shirt, they can have it. After all, they put it on my back to start with! They are fantastic – just crazy man. Everywhere I've played – they went wild. The difficulty comes when I leave the stage. It's im-possible now to leave my hotel room. I remember once I woke up in the night starving, but I didn't dare go out for any-thing. I tried it once, and the crowds were chasing me, and they smashed up an all-night delicatessen. In Atlantic City, they burst into my room – there were fifty of 'em in there. They grabbed hold of me, kissed me, and pulled my hair. They burst my bottom lip. In Kansas City I started to sing, and 6,000 of them ran for the stage. I escaped through a door, but they took the thing right off its hinges as they came after me. I ran into the back alley where the getaway car was wait-ing. One girl couldn't stop. She kept right on coming and coming, and ran her nose into the car door.'

Girls in the audiences, girls in the streets, in fact girls in general were a problem. The press were always asking ques-tions about them, and if Elvis dared to say more than two words to any particular dolly, he and she were practically en-gaged in the eyes of the reporters. 'You take a girl out twice and all of a sudden you are about to marry her. I enjoy dating girls more than anything. That's not wrong is it? They all think I'm a sex maniac. They're just frustrated old-types anyway. I'm just natural. I play the field. Why date one girl when there are so many beautiful girls around? Recently I've been paired off with Judy Spreckles. She's a member of the Spreckles Sugar family – it's a big company, everybody's heard of it. She gave me a 4 black star sapphire ring in Las Vegas. She was wearing my ring, I was wearing her ring. She's just like a sister to me!'

But it was more than a sister Elvis needed in Las Vegas when he was booked to appear at the Frontier Hotel in 1956. His show there was not what the grey haired old men with their secretaries wanted to see. 'I died a terrible death. When I came out with those hip movements, they just weren't ready for 'em.' Hip movements were the story line of the day, and Colonel Parker capitalised on even the bad publicity. One person who was obviously impressed with Elvis in Las Vegas was Hal Wallis, and despite his failure at the Frontier, Wallis invited Elvis to screen-test for him at Paramount. 'I can't thank Hal Wallis enough, for giving me this big break. I'm hoping to make good at whatever they give me to do. When I made my screen test, I didn't take a singing test, so I'm pleased because I wouldn't be interested in making movies if it just meant singing. What I want most of all is to be a good actor – it's my new ambition!'

Wallis reviewed the test and offered the rock 'n' roll star a three-film contract. When interviewed about the signing after a Wichita concert, Elvis' comments were later to be proved somewhat inaccurate. 'We've got a seven-year contract with Paramount. We'll have a movie comin' out – I don't know when, but we start making it in June. It's a movie with Burt Lancaster, and Katherine Hepburn called "The Rainmaker". I'd like to tell you how much we all appreciate this!' (In fact, Colonel Parker later refused the proposed role for Presley in 'The Rainmaker'. For Elvis to take the part of a somewhat demented young person was not what the Colonel had in mind for his protégé.) Strangely enough, Elvis' induction into the movies changed his speech. Hitherto he always referred to himself in the singular first person. Now, in fitting with his position perhaps, he was utilising the royal 'We'.

Elvis and the press were turning their attentions upon the Presley fleet of automobiles. An early count revealed three Cadillacs and a much sort after three-wheeled Messerschmitt, but these were now subject to continual change. On a give-away flexi-disc of the time Elvis said, 'I suppose you know I've got a lot of cars. People have written about it in the papers, and a lot of them ask and write and ask me why. Well, when I was driving a truck, every time a big shiny car drove by it started me sorta daydreamin', and I daydreamed about how it would be. The first car I ever bought was the most beautiful car I'd ever seen. It was second-hand, but I parked it outside my hotel, and sat up all night just looking at it. The next day the thing caught fire, and burned up on the road.' Now Elvis could also afford to move home, acquiring a ranch-house style property in the Audubon Park area of Memphis.

After he made a second appearance on the Milton Berle Television show in Los Angeles he signed to appear on the NBC Network for Steve Allen, this time from New York. Capitalising on the off-hand publicity, Allen thought that he would give America a new clean cut Elvis Presley. 'At the time Steve wanted to outdo the Ed Sullivan show on the other Network. Steve's got a weird mind. He dressed me in a tuxedo and tails, singing to a little fat hound dog perched on a stool. Not moving a muscle I had to sing to this fat little pooch, "You ain't nuthin' but a hound dog". For the whole show I couldn't move a muscle. Steve did that – I love him for it, but I'll never forgive him!' 'Hound Dog' was Elvis' new single release, and the sales of that single are again legendary. 'When I appeared on the show Steve Allen out-rated Ed Sullivan, and Ed sent a cable to Steve which simply said 'You rate!' Sullivan had previously said he would never use Elvis, but that week he began negotiations with the Colonel – for three shows.

Of all US TV light entertainment programmes, Ed Sullivan had the best in terms of both audience figures, and presentation. When Elvis appeared on his first Sullivan show, on September 9th, he notched up an all time record of 54 million viewers for the host. Ed Sullivan, a Richard Nixon look-a-like, welcomed Elvis on stage with the words 'America – Judge for yourself!'

America had been sitting in judgement for months. All over, groups of people were calling for one kind of restraint or another, and such upholders of public morality were later found to be up in arms when their demands were not implemented. Ed Sullivan had filmed Elvis from the waist up, in an attempt to prevent similar accusations being levelled against his show, but it wasn't sufficient to stop condemnation from the Catholic press. Elvis had already begun filming 'Love Me Tender' for Fox in Hollywood, and he used his Sullivan appearance as a springboard for the title track from the movies ... his latest single, though at the time he referred to the epic as being 'The Reno Brothers'. 'Love Me Tender' was one of eight singles released that week, seven were album track re-issues available for the first time to singles buyers. Because it was his first introduction to Hollywood, Elvis was determined to make a good impression. To that end he learned the entire script off by heart, but he was still very 'green' when it came to the film-makers tricks. When the young Presley fired a blank cartridge at his film brother Richard Egan Elvis almost collapsed in horror. As he fired the round, Egan clutched his 'bleeding' shoulder. Elvis rushed over to help only to find that the wound was caused by a little sack of studio 'blood' concealed under his clothing, which had been triggered off by an electric contact to coincide with the pistol shot. On the same set whilst Elvis was riding a horse under some trees, a low bough knocked him off, much to everyone's merriment. Only Elvis' pride was bruised, and the entire crew and cast warmed to the raw, young acting recruit.

Elvis' appearances on the film set were now giving visiting journalists more access to the new superstar. 20th Century Fox were anxious to give journalists as much freedom as possible because it was their investment Fox were protecting. These impromptu press conferences also gave Elvis the opportunity to express his feelings, and his on-set comments made up much of the back bone of most features written about him at the time. 'I don't like being called "Elvis The Pelvis". It's the most childish of expressions I've heard coming from an adult. Most adults, I find, are really kind. I've had them coming up to me and saying, "I personally don't like your music, but my kids do ..." Now they are adults with a little more intelligence than the others, and they take care not to run young people into the ground for simply having a nice time. My sideburns ain't comin off. I've been wearin' them since I was a kid. Truck drivers were my idols. In Tupelo and Memphis, I'd see those truck drivers wearing sideburns, and it was my ambition to look like them. I even got kicked off the school football team because of my sideburns, so we've both been through a lot together, and me and my sideburns are not partin'. A lot of bad things are being written about me and dope and such like. Let me tell you, I don't need anything to hop me up. Man, I need something to slow me down. Some people say I work too hard, but I guess that they are judging me on how much work they do, not on how much I feel like doing. Besides, I don't need much sleep – I get by on three hours – I think they call it nervous energy.

'I enjoy having my family around. I don't look on it as a duty – they can't be replaced – they are all I have in the world. My Mama says she hears me on the radio all day long. She and Daddy come to all of my shows within 100 miles of Memphis. In one way Mama can't take it very well, the girls mobbing me and all that. She thinks they are hurtin' me. I told her, "If you're gonna be like that, you'd better not come along, because that stuff is gonna keep right on happening – I hope."

'I'm real partial to good religious quartets like the Stamps and the Blackwood Brothers. I've liked that kind of music ever since I was a boy, and 'specially if there is a good bass singer. I'm gonna record some religious music one of these days. My favourite singers are Pat Boone, the Four Aces, Dean Martin, Tommy Sands, The Four Lads, and the Ames Brothers. My favourite actors and actresses include Marlon Brando, Rod Steiger, James Dean, Glenn Ford, John Wayne, Natalie Wood, Doris Day, and Kathryn Grayson.

'It's nice to have money. When I first began to get money, I bought a lot of things I'd always wanted, like cars. I kinda went mad. First one Cadillac, then another. Now I've bought my parents a new home, and my dad's been able to retire, and he's under 40! The way I look at it, Dad's worked hard all his life. It's time he had some enjoyment! I often ask myself "Why has this all happened to me?" My cousin, Gene Smith, and I often sit and talk about it. It seems only yesterday he and I were mowing lawns in Memphis.

'I'm flattered by the people who do impressions of me. You have to have a sense of humour in this business. When you start taking yourself seriously, you're in trouble. Sammy Davis does one of the best impersonations of me. I wouldn't presume to criticise a fellow artiste [Frank Sinatra had slammed Elvis at the time]. I don't think any artiste is in a position to ridicule another's accomplishments!'

Elvis broke off filming to return to his birth town in Mississippi. Tupelo had created an 'Elvis Presley Day', and the King was to perform on the stage at the Mississippi Alabama Fair and Dairy Show, the same platform he had used to expose his talents by singing 'Old Shep' thirteen years earlier. This time he received the freedom of the town, and five thousand dollars.

On 28th October Elvis made his second appearance on the Lincoln-Mercury Automobile sponsored Ed Sullivan Show. It was another sexual display which was to further divide the 'lovers' from the 'haters'. However, with huge audiences (around 80% of the nation's viewing public) the sponsors were pleased and presented him with a Lincoln after learning that he didn't possess one of their company's products. Back in Memphis Elvis was dating starlet Natalie Wood, his second album was released and he was soon to learn that the draft board was beginning to take an interest in him, although the board's chairman comforted fans by saying that there were hundreds scheduled to enlist before Elvis.

'Love Me Tender' was released on 17th November, being premiered at New York's Paramount Theatre. Huge crowds lined up outside the cinema for a movie which was to be number one box office material for the year, playing simultaneously at 550 selected locations. 'This is probably the greatest honour I've ever had in my life, though looking back I don't think it was the right part for me. The people at 20th Century Fox have been wonderful, they really helped us along, the stars, the director, and the producer. I didn't know one end of a camera from the other. I didn't think I was good at all, and worried about it. The studio helped me mostly by being so patient!'

Colonel Parker made sure that everything Elvis undertook would promote further activities. His second Ed Sullivan Show was a fine example. 'I'd like to tell you that on Thanksgiving Day, our new picture is to be released. Until we meet again, may God bless you, as he has blessed me.' On the day that 'Love Me Tender' was released, it was announced that 'Loving You', Elvis' second movie, this time for Paramount, was shortly to follow. Elvis started working on the film in December.

Just four days into 1957 Elvis was summoned to Kennedy Veterans Hospital in Memphis for a government physical examination. With him was a Las Vegas showgirl Dotty Harmony, and after the impromptu government sideshow Miss Harmony returned to Nevada, and Elvis headed to New York for the third and final Ed Sullivan telecast broadcast on January 9th. He told the viewing public: 'You made this the best Christmas we've ever had. We'd like to thank everybody for the Christmas presents, Christmas cards, and birthday cards. I got exactly 282 teddy bears! We're sorry that we couldn't give each one of you a new Lincoln, but they wouldn't sell us that many.' On the same day the Colonel called a press conference to announce that Elvis' third movie was to be 'Jailhouse Rock', this time for MGM.

At Paramount Elvis was assigned Anna Magnani's dressing room. 'Loving You' was previously going to be titled 'Lonesome Cowboy', but Elvis had objected. 'I'm not a cowboy singer. I sing hillbilly. I might wear dungarees, but that don't make me a cow-puncher. Hal Wallis has given me this film – he was the man who gave me my first screen test. I can't eat much, or my stomach'll show. Scotty, Bill, and DJ, are as skittish as colts when the cameras start rolling. You'd think they were tryin' for Acadamy Awards, instead of just doin' what comes naturally.'

The studio had to cope with 500 phone calls and 2,000 letters a day, many of which Elvis read, and even a few got answered during rare breaks in the hefty filming schedule. To get around the Paramount backlot Elvis used a bike, with 'Hound Dog' painted on it. He was known to hold races against the younger members of the film crew, and amused everyone with his prowess at trick cycling – an art he learned at school. Director Hal Kanter referred to Elvis as 'The Long Playing Fire-Cracker', and Elvis dubbed co-star Dolores Hart 'Whistle-britches'. It was a happy crew, and even Elvis' parents were involved on the set, teaching extras how to applaud in frenzy. 800 fans were invited to take part as extras in a night scene outside a theatre, but they needed no coaxing. In a fight scene Elvis fractured his 'wedding' finger, but avoided a more serious accident by side stepping a falling studio light. 'I met Charlton Heston at Paramount Studios. He was doing "The Ten Commandments", and he was always walking around our set dressed as Moses. He'd come into the dining room where I was eating and I'd holler "There's Moses". He was really nice!'

By mid-February Elvis was number one again, with 'Too Much'. It was his eighth 'million-seller', and by now every Presley platter was assured of a high chart position.

'Jailhouse Rock' was commenced at Culver City on May 1st. It was the first of many movies Elvis would make for MGM, and certainly one of his most memorable. He enjoyed the use of Bing Crosby's dressing room. Elvis had to rise each day at 6.30 am in time to arrive, made-up for action, on the sound stage by 8.30 am. Apart from a one hour break for lunch he would continue filming until 6.00 pm. In the evening Elvis would study the next day's script in his hotel room in Hollywood. For the part Elvis had to master the controls of an excavator for the opening scene, dance, and teach co-star Mickey Shaughnessy how to play guitar. (Ironically in the movie Shaughnessy had to show Elvis how to play chords.) The dance routines were choreographed by Alex Romero, and watched from the sidelines by Gene Kelly. Other visitors to the set included Paul Newman, Jean Simmons, and Russ Tamblyn. They had all come to watch Elvis do his 'Jailhouse Rock' number, and during the filming of this scene Elvis was to dislodge a newly fitted toothcap. It was later found in Elvis' lung, and he was hospitalised for its removal.

In another scene Elvis, who played the part of Vince Everett (a convict, falsely imprisoned, but singing his way to freedom) was called to read some fan mail. That was one piece of property which wasn't difficult to find, and actual Presley mail collected at the studio was used. During filming breaks Elvis dueted on piano with a fourteen-year-old beauty contest winner. Elvis received a cool quarter of a million dollars for the movie and had a royalty of 50% of the production's operating profits. 'I liked my role in "Jailhouse Rock", because it's the most dramatic part I've ever played. I felt that I was able to put myself into the place of the character I was playing, and feel his emotions.'

In July, after finishing at MGM, Elvis returned to Memphis. He spent much of his three-week vacation refurbishing a house he had bought three months earlier. It cost $100,000 and was situated in the Whitehaven district of the city, directly on Highway 51 (South). The estate was to be known as 'Graceland'.

Elvis was now to tour the Pacific North West, for the first time, and cross the border into Canada. On one Sunday, he played two concerts in two different cities – Tacoma and Seattle – some sixty miles apart. In those days Elvis didn't use a plane, and although a sixty-mile separation need only take an hour, more often than not it was a three-hour exercise. On September 1st Elvis crossed into Canada for his concert in Vancouver the same day. The venue was the Empire Stadium, where just a few years before Roger Bannister had broken the four-minute mile. The whole event was staged by Red Robinson, a slick sounding broadcaster who claimed to be the first DJ in Canada to play an Elvis record. Before the show (which Robinson also compered) the DJ spearheaded a thirty-minute press conference. So carried away with the sound of his own voice, Red Robinson preferred to ask and virtually answer each question he posed to the singing star, leaving Elvis just to answer 'Yes' or 'No'. Fortunately, many of the other interviewers present were more skilled in getting their subject to talk. During the pre-concert 'talk about' Elvis told the press about his early career, his $500 guitar, the bad press reports, his fans, and the usual subject, his sideburns. Elvis' love for cars also wasn't ignored. 'I had a German-made car, and there's a guy out there in town [Memphis] that's been waiting for that car for over a year. He owns a clothing store, one of the top clothes stores in Memphis, and so I went in there the other day and I told him, "You've been wanting the car so bad, I'll make a deal with you. Let me pick out all the clothes I want in here, and you can have the car!" He agreed. So I was in his store for almost two and a half hours. It was a wreck when I left.'

Before going on stage Elvis admitted that things were moving just a little too fast now, though he would sooner sing than be driving a truck. 'It was possibly the biggest crowd I've played to [26,000] second only to Dallas, Texas in 1956. I played the Cotton Bowl then, and I had some 32,000 people there!'

On Friday 27th September Elvis returned to Tupelo, Mississippi, for a benefit concert. All proceeds were donated to the 'Elvis Presley Recreational Centre' fund, and though advertised on bill posters weeks before, Elvis' back-up men Scotty Moore and Bill Black didn't appear. They resigned a week earlier over a pay and conditions disagreement.

After Tupelo, Elvis made his first visit to Hawaii. He was to make two appearances in the Honolulu Stadium, and the Colonel was waiting to supervise Elvis' arrival. Activities included two press conferences, firstly on the boat, and later, at the Hawaiian Village Hotel. 'I like having my friends along, it gives me a little touch of home! I like cars in loud colours and clothes in dark colours. I don't have a haircut very often, and when I do, it doesn't look like a haircut. I like "Don't Be Cruel" amongst my own records, and also the songs "You'll Never Walk Alone", and "Till". Rock 'n roll existed long before I did – it was called Rhythm and Blues. I just tried to give it a new interpretation. I feel an obligation to my fans, and I'm very careful not to do anything which might disappoint them. I behave myself all the time. People have preconceived ideas about me – it's natural. I've often said that I don't like a guy, but when I've got to know him he's really turned out to be nice. It's an easy mistake to make!'

Though the questions remained the same, Elvis was now

becoming more skilful in answering them, and in avoiding those impossible to deal with. But there were more press receptions looming over the horizon – on 20th December, after returning to Graceland for a family Christmas, Elvis received his government marching orders!

CHAPTER FIVE

'I'm kinda proud of it! It's a duty I've got to fill and I'm gonna do it. My induction notice says for me to leave my car at home – transportation will be provided. They tell me just to bring a razor, toothbrush, toothpaste, a comb, and enough money to hold me two weeks!'

So Elvis was to go into the US Army much earlier than everyone had wished. Paromount were busily putting together plans for 'King Creole' – an exercise which had already cost them $250,000 – and on-location filming was due to commence in New Orleans at the end of January 1958. However, that coincided with Uncle Sam's wishes. They wanted Elvis on January 20th, but so did Paramount. Consequently Elvis Presley was asked to write to the Draft Board stating the positions of all parties, and not unexpectedly an eight week deferment was granted.

'King Creole' is a Presley classic, and even Elvis' most loyal supporters wish that the star had continued movie making in the same vein. 'I'm not uncomfortable in this film. I enjoyed it. I felt that I was really acting, although I'm a prisoner to my tonsils. I guess my fans would expect me to sing no matter what. For the first time I'm playing someone other than "Elvis Presley". I don't think the boy in the story "A Stone for Danny Fisher" would wear long sideburns, and that's why I had them shaven off.'

Much of the filming was on location in and around the night club areas of New Orleans' notorious French Quarter. Guided tour leaders still point out the schoolyard where a Presley brawl was staged, and the night club which was used as the 'King Creóle' in the story. 'I remember my first time in the city. I played to 75 people. Man, there were more folks on stage than in the audience. I had to borrow the car fare the next day to get to my next date in Shreveport. However our next concert there was different. We had some 13,000 people to entertain.' Elvis responded well to Michael Curtiz's film direction. After the final scene was shot, the cast threw a surprise party which lasted all night. Actress Dolores Hart gifted Elvis with an antique musket, and starlet Valerie Allen completed his collection of pre-army going away presents with a pack of corn plasters.

At the crack of dawn, on Monday 24th March, Elvis presented himself at his local Draft Board offices. Again he was accompanied by Judy Spreckles and his parents. Lamar Fike, his companion, tried to enlist at the same time, but was refused for being overweight. Another fatty was there too, Colonel Parker of course, anxious to use every minute to publicise 'King Creole'. After the medical, the oath was taken and the King of Pop became US Army Private Number 53310761. Upon his induction a US fan club president presented Elvis with a box containing a banana cream pie and a bible, and Elvis with seven volunteers and thirteen other draftees boarded a bus for Fort Chaffee, Arkansas. The Colonel was there too, to pull rank on the 'real' officers, and to make sure that his boy was getting everything he required. He ensured that the press got every picture they wanted, though no-one got the locks of hair which Elvis paid some 65 cents to have removed by the Army barber.

'I'm A–1. It'll be quite a drop from $10,000 a month, but I'll manage. I guess the only thing I'll hate about it is leaving Mama. She's always been my best girl. I won't ask any special favours. I want to be treated no different from the other boys. I don't want to go into the "Special Services". I hope my fans will welcome me back. Maybe I'll start a new career in two years time as a ballad singer, or a singer of spirituals.' At one time it was considered by Colonel Parker that a move into the 'Special Services' would be a good one for Elvis. Most of the cream of the entertainment field were serving in the Army's entertainment units, and such service was encouraged by the Army generals. In fact even after the Colonel had said 'no' and Elvis had echoed his wishes, the Army did everything to dissuade Elvis from the normal draftee's service.

On Thursday a press conference was called to announce

that Elvis would take his basic training at Fort Hood, in Texas, with the Second Armoured Division. 'You name it, I've been all over Texas. I got my start in music around Houston. The other guys have been swell to me. The only GIs I've seen so far are those around the barracks. They treat me the same as anyone else, and that's the way I want it! I suppose it's the natural thing when a fella goes to a strange place is to try and find a girl.'

The next morning they were off, followed by the 55 newsmen and photographers who were witnessing Elvis' every move for his first week of Army life. Two days later they were told that enough was enough, and that Elvis was to start being a proper soldier. 'Man, I've never been so scared of anything in my life. I'm not used to guns. I spent most of my time inside camp. There was every kind of sport, craft and so on. We were never stuck for anything to do. I went to the camp cinema quite often, and I talked to my folks on the phone two or three times a week – that was a necessity. The first eight weeks were murder. I ended up exhausted, but I felt good. I lost 8 lbs in weight, but got it back in solid muscle.'

Elvis was now granted two weeks leave, and he used his time to visit Nashville to record a few new songs – tracks which were to become precious as the months passed, and in-the-can material dried up. After the session followed the usual round of parties, and after the fun Elvis headed back to Fort Hood.

His parents followed, and being dependent relatives, were able to live off camp with Elvis in a three-bedroomed house in Killean. Colonel Parker had studied the Army regulations, and was overjoyed when it was found that Elvis could live off camp if his parents lived in the area.

However, the delight was short lived. Gladys Presley had been ill for some time, and on August 8th, she and her husband Vernon returned to Memphis to consult the family doctor. She was immediately admitted into hospital, and three days later Elvis was summoned to Memphis. Compassionate leave was granted and Elvis and his father took it in turns to sit by her bedside. On August 14th she died, and doctors recorded that death was attributed to a heart attack.

'I remember, when she felt bad, we'd walk her down the driveway to help her feel better. Oh God, everything I had is gone. She's all we lived for!' After the funeral Elvis remained in Memphis until Sunday August 24th when he flew to Dallas. 'One of the last things Mom said was that Dad and I should always be together. I'll report back to Fort Hood in the morning, and wherever they send me, Dad will come too. Before I went home, I was scheduled to leave for Germany about 1st September; Mom and Dad had often talked about Europe. I'll guess we'll go there now – the two of us.'

On September 1st 350 troops, including Elvis headed, by train, to Brooklyn. They were to join the SS General Randal for the sea journey to Germany and Colonel Parker was on hand, with Steve Sholes of RCA to supervise the operation. RCA were there in force to record the press conference which was later issued almost in full on an EP entitled 'Elvis Sails'. It sold a million, of course. 'I'm looking forward to Germany. I'm looking forward to seeing the country and meeting the people, but at the same time I'm looking forward to coming home. I'll do whatever the Army tells me to do, and I've been looking forward to going abroad. We were actually planning a world tour before I knew exactly when I would be going into the Army. My fan mail has doubled since I've been in the service. And I have to thank my high-school pre-military training for making it a little easy for me – you see I already knew my right leg from the left one. The first place I'll go to see when I get a pass is Paris!' After 'all visitors ashore', the military brass band played 'Hound Dog' and the vessel slipped slowly out of port for an uneventful month long sailing to Bremerhaven.

As soon as she docked, all were quickly transferred by train to their new encampment in Friedberg, a small town not far from Frankfurt. The Army played host to the press yet again, but by October 5th the barracks were 'off limits' to all visitors. When Elvis' family joined him, he was allowed to live off-camp, firstly in a hotel, and following hard negotiations with the owner, in a four-bedroomed house at Goethestrasse 14, Bad Nauheim.

'I'm getting to like the Army. I'm in a scout platoon; we

draw routes for tanks and heavy machinery – it's quite a change from singing. I get to the post around 6.00 am and return to our house at 6.00 pm. I have dinner with my Dad, my grandmother and some friends (by now two of Elvis' Memphis companions Red West and Lamar Fike were living with Elvis' family). We have our house on the outskirts of the town, and we love it. My grandmother cooks all my favourite dishes – you know, simple food, just like my Mama used to make. I'm getting around 15,000 letters a week now, but apart from the few I'm able to answer, the Colonel's office takes care of them. I've bought a new guitar. When I get time off I love to drive my new white German sports car. You should see me go on those autobahns. I plan to come to England as soon as I can – possibly in 1961. I saw those white cliffs of Dover on the way over here, and I'd sure like to see them again. Every day when I wake up there's a lot of people at the gate. They come from all over Germany and Europe, and bring their families at weekends, and take pictures and everything.'

So intense was the interest in Elvis' German home that to prevent damage, waiting fans were consoled with a newly erected door sign which read 'Autographs only between 6.30 pm and 7.00 pm please'.

Meanwhile, outside of his army life, Elvis was continuing to dominate the world's hit parades with a mixture of re-released album tracks spiced occasionally with a treasured new single. 'King Creole' made the cinema rounds, and was highly acclaimed by the critics, and movie-goers were able to enjoy re-runs of his three earlier pictures. It's quite remarkable to realise that although Elvis was away from his public for two years, only two months passed when there was no Elvis material in the US singles charts.

Back in Germany, Elvis was seen to be making the most of his Army life. He became a blood donor in January of 1959 giving his precious drops to the German Red Cross. Off duty he dated Margrit Buergin and another starlet Vera Tchecova, and eventually met Priscilla Beaulieu – the 14-year-old daughter of an Air Force captain. (Vernon Presley met his new wife in Germany. She was at the time married to an Army soldier.) Elvis bought a brown French poodle and called it 'Champagne', and the keys of his white BMW were given to him in a small ceremony (for the press) by Germany TV personality Uschi Seibert. At weekends, Elvis would play touch football with his army buddies, breaking a finger on one occasion, and once he actually ventured to a football match guarded by two Military Police.

In June Elvis went to Paris. He had promised himself a trip to the French capital, and he was delighted with what he saw. 'It reminded me of the life I used to live, before I joined the service. I loved Paris. I didn't have to sign too many autographs, and I became an ordinary guy for a while. I enjoyed the break – I needed the rest!'

During his two-week stay at the exclusive Prince of Wales Hotel, Elvis ventured out often. Once he went to the Lido, and became noticed as being the only person drinking tomato juice when all around him were supping champagne. On another night at the cabaret club, he stayed on after the audience left, and gave an impromptu concert for the benefit of cleaners, waiters, and the like. He accompanied himself on piano singing quiet songs including 'Willow Weep For Me'. 'For the first time in fifteen months, there I was in front of an audience. I play quite a bit at my house, singing at the piano for my friends, but here was a live audience and then it flew all over me, boy – sudden fear!'

Elvis' unpublicised Paris 'concert' was possibly his only 'appearance' throughout his Army career. The Colonel had insisted that there were to be no Army concerts, but the veto didn't prevent certain generals pursuing the matter further at every available opportunity. 'I was just another human being in the Army. I couldn't be in showbusiness and the Army too. I told them, "Gentlemen, I have no instruments!" I'd been in the service for over a year, and I said it would be difficult for me to bring my musicians over to Germany. I didn't want to start performing after a year. My army friends had accepted me for what I was, and I didn't want to go back on anything – they had really opened my whole perspective. I was glad I could come into the Army, and while I'm in I'll concentrate on soldiering. Though, I'll be happy to return to the entertainment world, because once you get a taste of showbusiness there's really nothing like it.'

Throughout the summer Hal Wallis and Paramount

Pictures were in Germany filming advanced location shots for Elvis' first post-Army movie. Originally titled 'Cafe Europa', it was decided not to use Elvis in any way whilst he was still serving his country, and consequently a stand-in, Mr T. W. Creel, was used. The movie later had the now world renowned title 'GI Blues'.

Quite a lot of journalists visited Elvis during his off duty moments, and he'd frequently talk about the music which was moulding his own outlook. 'I still sing rock 'n' roll, though I love to sing songs like "I'll take you home again, Kathleen". I'm beginning to love mood music, and Irish tenors. If nothing else this stay in Europe has really brought me up to date with European music styles. I've heard a lot of it, and I like it.'

In the new year (1960) Elvis returned to Paris, and was promoted to sergeant. He had learned to shoot so straight that he was the only one on camp who could light a match with a single pistol shot. It was the tail end of his Army service. On March 1st Elvis attended at farewell press conference at Ray Barracks, Friedberg. Ironically the event was staged by Captain Marion Keisker — the girl who had first taken an interest in Elvis' voice at Sun Records. 'Marion! In Germany! And you're an officer! What do I do? Do I kiss You or salute You?' Army chiefs were liberal in their praise of Elvis, and he was awarded a special citation certificate.

It was also said that Elvis had kept only one dollar of his weekly Army pay, donating the rest to charity. 'I guess it won't be too difficult adjusting from $80 to $1 million! But it won't be too easy adjusting my life style. I've lost about 10 lbs and I tip the scales at 170 lbs. I didn't get into any fights, because the Army played it straight, and so did I. Firstly, I'm going home to do a television show with Frank Sinatra, and then I'll make some films. I hope they will not all be rock 'n' roll movies. I've made four of those already, and you know, you can only get away with doing the same thing for so long. I'm not going to have my tonsils out. It'll possibly make me sing too good. I'd like to develop my acting career, tackling a role similar to Mr Sinatra when he made "From Here to Eternity". I'm gonna let my sideburns grow a little, but I doubt if they'll be as long as they were – I've got over that kick. I'll just continue doing what comes naturally. I don't consider the new crop of singers as rivals. I've always believed that there's room for everyone in showbusiness. I don't know about marriage. I guess I'll wait until the bug bites, and it hasn't yet. I've been seeing a lot of Priscilla Beaulieu and I've dated her often. She is very mature, very intelligent, and the most beautiful girl I've ever seen. But there's no romance, it's nothing serious!' The following day Elvis boarded an Army plane at Frankfurt, pausing briefly in the swirling snow to wave goodbye to cameramen and Priscilla. The plane touched down at Prestwick Airport in Scotland for an hour, and after another round of autographs, the party headed off into the sky bound for McGuire Airbase in New Jersey, USA.

On March 3rd Elvis and his party landed in another blizzard, and Miss Nancy Sinatra was there to greet him, with a gift – a couple of shirts made for him by her father's tailor. Elvis was transferred to the adjacent Fort Dix army post for a further round of questions from the press. 'Sobering Army life? No it hasn't changed my mind about rock 'n' roll Besides, I was in tanks and they rock 'n' rolled quite a bit. I like American girls and German girls – they're all female! Priscilla, my date, has to stay out in Germany with her family for another three years. I'm gonna stay in showbusiness – the Colonel would shoot me if he thought I was going to quit! I might be a bit rusty, but I practised a lot in Germany. I had some instruments and a tape recorder – don't worry, I'll be in there fighting!'

On the 5th March Elvis Presley, Sergeant US Army, became a civilian again, and the world sighed!

'Before I was drafted, things just kept snowballing. I had no time to stop and think. The Army gave me that time. The Army taught me about liberty, freedom, and teamwork. It also gave me time to read some good books, and contemplate on the more serious aspects of living.'

CHAPTER SIX

'After two years isolation, it was sorta strange at first. But after singing for a couple of hours, it all came natural again. Rock 'n' roll has to be natural. The audience can tell if it's faked!'

Elvis' arrival back in Memphis caused the usual hullabaloo. Local radio networks pumped out 24 hours of non-stop Presley, and even the big store in town, 'Goldsmiths' took a full page ad in the local rag proclaiming Elvis' homecoming. Gary Pepper, a local fan club secretary, crippled by cerebral palsey, greeted Elvis at the Memphis railroad terminal. Elvis was visibly moved to tears. (Pepper had originally taken interest in Elvis from the time he used to operate a stars' newspaper cutting service. Most would send him $5 for each batch of clippings. When he sent Elvis his first selection he sent Gary a $50 bank note.) To celebrate his home coming Elvis bought himself a present. 'When I got out of the Army in 1960 I bought myself a [black] Rolls Royce. I remember, I was driving it in Beverley Hills one day, and Jerry Lewis pulled up beside me. He looked over and so did I. He called my manager the same day and said "Tell Elvis not to drive a Rolls Royce without a tie on." I will give you a couple of guesses to the message I sent in reply!'

A recording session had been booked for Jim Reeves at RCA's Nashville studios on March 20th, though people became suspicious when an order for 100 hamburgers and french fries was received at the Crystal Hamburger house. The girls guessed it was Elvis. Six songs were recorded in the eleven-hour session, including 'Stuck on You' and 'Fame and Fortune'. Then Elvis was off to Miami – to guest on the Frank Sinatra show. The 700 strong audience consisted of a mixture of elite ladies and their daughters. In his Army uniform Elvis nervously sang a line of 'It's Nice to Go Travelling'. 'My movements weren't natural – I was shaking. I wasn't just nervous, I was petrified!' However a much more relaxed Elvis sailed through his new release 'Stuck on You', and 'Fame and Fortune', and he dueted with Sinatra on 'Witchcraft' whilst the latter tackled 'Love Me Tender'. The show was taped and broadcast to a 50% scoop audience on May 12th.

After the show recording, Elvis returned to Nashville to cut his first ever 'stereo' album 'Elvis Is Back' – even the album covers were printed before the final track selection was known in order to fill demand in the stores around America. 'Stuck on You', the single premiered at the Sinatra taping, hit the top of the charts, selling against advanced orders of a million and a half.

On 21st April Elvis reported to Paramount in Hollywood. 'The story of GI Blues takes place in Germany, but it's not about my actual experiences in the Army – they couldn't film that!' However, the star was to give technical help on more than one occasion. For instance, when an M48 slipped its track, Elvis was able to repair the tank, and filming could continue. Royalty watched the filming from the sidelines in the shape of three European Princesses, the King and Queen of Nepal, and the Thai Royal Household. Other visitors to the set were Dean Martin, Lawrence Harvey, and Shirley MacLaine. Elvis, who had been given Lana Turner's dressing room, threw a wild party to celebrate Dean's birthday.

'At the time we were filming GI Blues I had just received my first degree black belt in karate. Between takes we were working out, breaking boards, tiles, and bricks. You know, generally showing off, though at the time I called it "demonstrating". And I blocked a kick the wrong way. Then I had to do a love scene with a guitar and Juliet Prowse – and there was this big fat hand. They tried to camouflage it with make-up, but there was nothing they could do – it looked like it belonged to another person. It even came out on the album – have a look at the back of it, it looks like somebody blew it up. I enjoyed the scenes in GI Blues where I had to babysit. I really like children. When I marry, I'd like four or five children.'

About this time US newspapers were rife with reports of an

impending marriage between Vernon Presley and Devada Stanley, the woman he met in Germany during Elvis' two-year army stint. It was said that Elvis was to be best man, but Elvis didn't attend the ceremony on 3rd July at Huntsville Alabama. 'If I had gone to the wedding, everyone would have turned up looking for stories. Everywhere I go it becomes some sort of a circus, and as I think a wedding should be a sacred thing, I didn't attend. She realises she will never take the place of my mother – no-one will, but she seems very nice. My dad was a good husband, and never left my mother's side in 26 years. If he has found happiness again, I'm very happy for him. I call her Dee, and I have a lot of respect for her!'

With 'GI Blues' completed in August of 1960, Elvis moved across to 20th Century Fox to make 'Flaming Star'. In the movie Elvis offered his audience one of his finest characterisations, playing the part of a half breed red-skin experiencing resentment from both the Indian and the white man. Director Don Seigal noted that after fight screens the star was visibly angry – Elvis staged his own fights, and never using a stand-in. Actor Rodd Redwing coached Elvis in the art of 'quick-draw'.

Co-starring in the movie, originally titled 'Flaming Lance', was veteran actress Dolores Del Rio, still displaying the finer points of her earlier sophisticated beauty. 'Dolores is a real nice person, and a great actress. I'm honoured at being permitted to work with her. We had to work on location shots all through September on a ranch just outside of Los Angeles. We had to get up at 5.00 am and work right through till 6 o'clock in the evening.'

Although Elvis was to spend almost all of his working time in Hollywood, there was no record of him joining the social scene or becoming a member of the 'party-set'. 'I think people in Hollywood have feelings, but most of them are too wrapped up in their careers and hold their emotions in reserve until success comes. That's why I find it difficult to get to know them. I don't hit the glamour spots, unless it's to see a friend working – like Bobby Darin at Cloisters. If I started going to parties I would have to go to them all, so I prefer to stay at

46

my hotel, and have my parties here. There's always a lot of people coming and going, and we sit and play records, eat food and drink Cokes. Back home I even rent the fairground or a cinema, and let everyone roam loose and have a good time. I enjoy going to the movies, and I'm a big reader of poetry. Thinking of the future, what I'd really like to do is take that long awaited foreign tour. It would finally give me the opportunity to actually meet some of the people who have been so wonderful to me on the other side of the Atlantic.'

Once again Elvis was firmly entrenched in the singles and album charts. At the time 'It's Now or Never', a song based on the Italian operetta piece 'O Sole Mio', held on to the number one position for weeks, and occupied a chart placing for almost a year. 'I was still in the Army when it was suggested that I should update the song. I thought the idea was nuts – a lovely song like that deserved respect. I'm pleased with how it turned out – my biggest all time seller!'

With his second post-Army movie completed, Elvis Presley headed for home. 'Graceland is full of memories for me. Maybe that's what makes it home. I always dreamed of it while I was in the Army. I first bought it for my mother, and when she died it seemed empty. It was quite a while before I wanted to come back, though as soon as I was discharged, that's where I was headed. When my father re-married, he moved into his own place, but it's not far away – just around the corner, and I still see him often. I have my pals staying at Graceland. We swim and play football.'

It was during a football knock-about that again Elvis broke a finger, and he spent his first ever night in the newly built Baptist Hospital. Who would have guessed that it was to become a frequent retreat for him ten or so years later? Still, visit number one was a pleasant experience, especially for the kids in the children's ward. In the morning one of Elvis' friends, Joe Esposito, chauffeured him home. 'Joe is an old Army buddy. When I got demobbed, I offered him a job. Now he travels with me – I like the company. Usually I have six or seven travelling with me, most of them friends from back home, about my age. They are not bodyguards. One is my accountant, another my travel consultant. I need a valet, a security officer, and a wardrobe man with me almost all the time. I don't like them being referred to as the "Memphis Mafia" – I prefer to look on them as members of a little "country-club" that I run.'

Elvis finished off his year by returning to Hollywood to make his final movie for Fox. It was 'Wild in the Country', and another strong acting role, although fans were disappointed at the lack of the usual dozen songs. One has to remember that at the time fans could only see Elvis perform his million sellers on the silver screen, and no matter how outdated they may appear today, at the time they were received with equally outdated clichés such as 'wowsville' from cinema audiences who had possibly queued five hours for a seat.

Being teetotal, Elvis had to be coached in acting in a drunken manner, and from his performance, someone possibly had to spike his Coke. Another 'abstainer', British DJ Jimmy Savile, O.B.E., was to visit the set to present Elvis with an award for his first UK million seller, the single 'It's Now or Never', and returned to England with wonderful tales of his meeting with the superhuman being. As Jimmy tells it, 'The Colonel said, "Bring a picture man," and lo and behold, I finished up with a picture of me and El standing side by side shaking hands. The first ever picture of a British person ever in contact with the guy, shakin' hands with 'im. It might mean nothing now, but then it was an unbelievable world-beating thing. So I flew back with the picture, had a lot of 'em printed, and sold 'em. We raised £150 – which was a lot of money in those days – which I took to Buckingham Palace and donated it to the Duke of Edinburgh's Playing Fields Association Fund!' Whilst Elvis was nick-naming his co-star 'Thursday' Weld, and singing folk songs that he said RCA wouldn't allow him to record, the press were buzzing with reports of his dates with wardrobe mistress Miss Nancy Sharpe.

1961 started with a bang, spearheaded with Elvis' return to live appearances. The year was to be one of his finest, with the release of four of his most popular films reaching cinema audiences around the world, and mammoth chart successes. 'Are You Lonesome Tonight', 'Wooden Heart' (Britain only),

'Surrender', 'Wild In The Country', and 'His Latest Flame' all became international number one records!

In February Elvis gave two charity performances at the Ellis Auditorium in Memphis. The Governor proclaimed 25th February 'Elvis Presley day' throughout the State of Tennessee, and Elvis was honoured at a special luncheon at the Claridge Hotel for world wide record sales in excess of 75 million units. The two concerts netted $50,000, part of which went at Elvis' request to children's charities in Tupelo, and the remainder to various Memphian funds. (Elvis Presley has always supported good causes and annually donates a sum to each of thirty-five Memphis charities. In total this has often been reported to be as high as $100,000. It's also widely understood that a portion of his annual income (some say $2\frac{1}{2}\%$) is given to the Actors Benevolent Fund.) At the pre-concert press reception Elvis admitted that he was readying himself for greater things.

'I would like to play dramatic roles, but I'm not ready for it quite yet. And eventually I'll have to do a European tour – because of all the people over there; though Colonel Parker could answer that better. I don't smoke, though occasionally I smoke a cigar if the Colonel gives me one – which is not very often. I'm superstitious, especially about photographers, and breaking mirrors and the like, I hope always to live in Memphis, and my favourite disc is *It's Now or Never*. I'm too tied up with movies to do any more TV.' The usual questions and the usual replies, but the concerts were far from usual. Elvis was dressed in a white sports jacket, and black trousers, as he sang his way through some twenty songs starting with 'Heartbreak Hotel' and including 'Don't', 'Swing Low Sweet Chariot', 'Such A Night' – the hit of the performance – and finishing on 'Hound Dog'.

A few days later, on March 8th, Elvis was made an honorary Tennessee 'Colonel' and received the commission at a specially convened meeting of the General Assembly of the Tennessee Legislature in Nashville. 'I'm sorry I can't sing or play for you, and that I'm not as funny as Tennessee Ernie Ford, who I understand was here last week. Except when I had my sideburns – then I was pretty funny! This is one of the

49

nicest things that's happened to me in my career. God bless you all, as he has blessed me!'

After the function, Elvis stayed on in Nashville to record, before flying out to Hawaii for a charity performance on 25th March at the Bloch Arena where he raised $62,000 for the USS 'Arizona' memorial fund. His Pan Am jet clipper was met by 3,000 screaming fans at Honolulu Airport, and he faced questions from thirty high school junior reporters at a special press reception, hosted by the local press council. It was a charity 'do' all right – with everyone including Elvis having to buy a ticket. 'If I gotta pay to get on the stage to sing, then that's good enough for me.' Elvis stayed on the island after the concert to film location scenes for Paramount's 'Blue Hawaii'.

'It's a comedy-romance type of thing with a lot of action with girls on Waikiki beach. I play a guy called Chad Gates who returns home from the army after a two-year hitch to Honolulu, determined not to follow his mother's wishes, that of a job in the family pineapple business, and to settle down and marry a girl equal to his own social position. My first assignment in the film is to act as escort to four girls and their teacher around the islands – I guess you can figure it out from there!'

When all the locations were completed Elvis returned to Hollywood, and was given Marlene Deitrich's Paramount dressing room. 'I think Miss Deitrich is the most eternally beautiful and feminine woman in the world. It's nice to have her dressing room, especially as it has its own kitchen facilities. I like to cook up eggs and very crisp bacon or ham for my lunch. Several times while on location in Hawaii I would have easily traded some of their super hospitality for a little cookin' – Tennessee style! I enjoy location work, but it would make a change being a tourist, instead of a tourist attraction. I'd like to see Big Ben, and go roaming in the hills of Scotland.'

When Elvis was confronted with reporters on the set he said that his musical tastes had improved in recent months. 'Now I have every kind of record from early Caruso to modern day hill-billy. I still prefer spiritualist singers like Mahalia

Jackson.' When quizzed on possible Las Vegas work he replied 'I doubt if I'll ever work in nightclubs – I don't like 'em!'

Filming over, Elvis returned home. His outside activities had expanded to include sailing – he bought three boats – but once stayed out on the lake too long, caught tonsillitis and was ill for three days. Other hobbies were now to include go-karting and shooting. He bought a pet monkey and called it 'Skatter', and formed a football squad and named the team 'Elvis Enterprises'. Escorting Anita Wood to the ceremony, he attended a wedding between Red West (a long standing employee), and Pat Boyd (another employee – his secretary) on 1st July. 'Marriage is nice – but I'm not ready for it yet!'

The movie machine was now in full swing. With making at least three, sometimes four movies each year, Elvis had little time to himself. Following another Nashville session it was time again to move home, this time to Florida, as the Mirisch Film Company descended on Crystal Lake for 'Follow That Dream'. Elvis had a new red Cadillac, and fitted with air-conditioning it made a welcome retreat, away from the sultry climate of the area. This new 'prop' was used in the production, driven by payroll buddy Lamar Fike, as he sped the movie 'governor' along a new road for the official opening ceremony. Elvis interrupted his location work to be crowned 'King' during Tampa's Latin Festival, accompanied by 4,000 teenagers; and then moved to Hollywood to work on the 'inside' shots. 'I had a wonderful time doing "Follow That Dream". We spent a lot of time during breaks throwing fish at each other. Arthur O'Connel, my pa in the film ... what he taught me!!!!!'

In the Autumn Elvis grew a moustache, but quickly shaved it off before returning to Hollywood for 'Kid Galahad', a boxing movie set in the mountains at Idyllwild, some way from Los Angeles. A year earlier, in England, a Derbyshire print shop worker started a magazine called *Elvis Monthly*. Though it was first published some five years after the outbreak of Elvis Presley's career, Albert Hand found he was satisfying an enormous demand, an available market hitherto ignored by the publishing magnates. No-one previously considered it possible to produce a magazine, on a regular basis, solely devoted to one artiste. Albert was a pioneer, and although he died in his early forties, in April 1972, the periodical is still produced and is soon to enjoy its twentieth year of publication, and outliving its contemporaries *The Rolling Stones Monthly* and *The Beatles Book*.

Albert Hand (who was later to take over the British Presley Fan Club from its original founders) met Elvis on location, a friendly meeting arranged by Colonel Parker, Vernon Presley and Decca UK, the then licensors of the RCA product for Great Britain. On set Elvis said to him: 'We came out here at about 6.00 am, but we can't do any filming until the sun comes out. You see "Kid Galahad" is supposed to take place in mid-summer, and before we started filming the "Kwimpers" thing (an earlier title for "Follow that Dream") I said, "Why not film 'Kid Galahad' in the mountains first, and then 'Follow That Dream' in the winter in Florida when it's still warm." They didn't go much on the idea, so here we are, waitin' for the sun to come out, and all slowly freezing to death. "Pioneer Go Home" (Follow That Dream) is the best film I've ever done. It's the funniest and strangely it didn't start out that way. I enjoyed Europe, but I didn't see enough of it. But one day I'll go back and make up for all the things I missed seeing the first time 'round. This place reminds me of Germany, the hills, the trees, it's beautiful. I hope you'll all like "Blue Hawaii" when it's released over in England – I think you'll have to see the film to appreciate it fully, especially the "Hawaiian Wedding Song" scene. It must sound funny hearing the sound-track album before seeing the film. They do funny things with sound-tracks. Cuttin' things out, and puttin' things in. Take "Flaming Star" for instance. When we made that it had four songs – I thought they should all go out. In the end they did cut two of 'em. They even had me singing one of those cut out, sitting on horseback. I think it was called "Breeches" or something – thank heaven they cut that one out.'

Elvis missed out on his usual Memphis Christmas, but he arrived back home in January 1962 for recording in Nashville, and a brief interlude between movie-making. In the spring he and his usual all-male entourage headed out to Hawaii for a film originally titled 'Cumbo Ya Ya' and set in New Orleans, now re-titled 'Welcome Aboard', and to be changed yet again to 'A Girl in Every Port', before finally being released on the cinema circuits as 'Girls, Girls, Girls!'

When Elvis arrived at Honolulu Airport he was met by an even bigger crowd than before. Some 8,000 people had turned out to greet the man who was fast becoming a legend on the islands. His personal kindnesses, and continual praise for the Hawaiian peoples brought in return enormous respect and admiration. They were even more grateful for his charitable appearances the previous year and the publicity the Island Paradise was enjoying through his movies. Much of the action was shot along the Kona Coastline of the main island Hawaii, and Elvis, encouraged by the atmosphere generated by off-camera extras dancing whenever he sang, helped to make the movie a popular favourite. Reporters visiting the Hollywood set of 'Girls, Girls, Girls!' still posed the marriage question, but Elvis went to great lengths to stress that he wasn't in-volved, and added that it was now getting more difficult to spot a girl who wanted him solely for himself.

'I've had close family ties all my life, so I want to settle down like any normal guy and have kids.' Elvis also admitted to wearing a disguise in an attempt to go out by himself with-out being killed in the rush. Elvis' fear of flying was the re-peatedly reported reason for him not touring outside of the confines of the United States, although many forgot that although Hawaii was USA territory, to reach it you had to fly. He preferred to remain in the States, and as if to emphasise his dislike of air travel he bought a mobile home which was used for a while to transport him between Memphis and Hollywood. The journey was about 2,000 miles and it took Elvis and his boys several arduous days driving, so consequently the novelty of this acquisition soon wore off. As if to add in-sult to injury, Elvis' next role portrayed him as a flyer in 'It Happened at the World's Fair'. MGM filmed much of the location footage at Seattle during the actual event, and the crowds delighted in seeing Elvis in action. The visitors were also 'used' as unpaid extras, just one of the advantages of film-ing at an international event. Back in Culver City, Samuel

Goldwyn gifted Elvis with a suite of rooms within the MGM film lot, which were still used up until early 1977 as Colonel Parker's West Coast base-office. (The Colonel, who today lives in Palm Springs, now operates from within the RCA Complex on Sunset Boulevard in Hollywood.)

During the making of 'It Happened at the World's Fair' Elvis Presley was invited to appear before Her Majesty, Queen Elizabeth II, at the annual British Royal Variety Performance. His refusal (although he did send a donation to the charitable fund) angered the British press, and no amount of excuses were able to repair the damage caused by the affront. It was reported at the time that the Colonel had conditionally agreed to meet the royal request, only if his star was guaranteed to meet Her Majesty. When such an application was refused Parker commented, 'If the Queen doesn't want to meet Elvis, then we have no right to be there!' One is led to believe that a more diplomatic approach from both sides would have clinched the appearance ... but it was not to be. Though the year ended with a world-wide number one with the 'Return To Sender', it was obvious that the royal request refusal soured an otherwise perfect year. It was certainly a bad omen, as the years to follow were never to be as successful as 1962.

CHAPTER SEVEN

'I've got every record the Beatles have ever made.
I've heard about the Rolling Stones, but I haven't
heard their records yet!'

The new year brought a new kind of prosperity to the British
people. The Liverpool sound was taking off on both sides of
the Atlantic, and because of their export achievements the
Beatles were later to be awarded Royal honours. The music
capitals of the world turned their attentions upon the British
music industry much to the detriment of the established American acts. Within a year Britain's coastline was to be surrounded
by a fleet of pirate radio stations, and 'Swinging England' was
the order of the day. From 1963 onwards Elvis' success could
only be measured by the chart placing of his latest single.

Elvis entered the new year hot on the heels of news that his
long time romance with Anita Wood was terminated. But there
was work to do, and in the usual way he reported to Hollywood
to make 'Fun In Acapulco'. Though the flimsy story-line was
set in Acapulco Elvis never went on location, because, it was
reported, he was outlawed in Mexico. Consequently stand-ins
were used, whilst Elvis and curvy co-star Ursula Andress
battled with a tame script at the studio's Hollywood sound
stages. 'After this film I'll be going on vacation to Memphis,
then the next movie will be "The Magic Touch" for MGM
with Ann-Margret. I'm looking forward to this, especially going on location, as I like Las Vegas very much.'

Elvis' holiday kicked off the second round of his courtship
with pretty Miss Beaulieu. Her parents had sent Priscilla to
Memphis in advance of their return from Germany, and Elvis
said that she was staying at Graceland as a house guest of the
Presley family, whilst continuing her studies at the Immaculate
Conception High School.

Elvis also used his time to record at Nashville, which turned

55

out to be his last intensive non-film soundtrack session for three years. (Most film soundtracks were taped in Hollywood, though Elvis returned to Nashville for the songs from 'Kissin Cousins' in an attempt to recapture the country-sound.)

$3,000,000 had been budgeted for 'Viva Las Vegas', and with this above average sum the producers were able to attract the services of a delicious co-star! 'I regard Ann-Margret as just about the most exciting new find in recent years!' She was popular too with Elvis Presley's fans, with sex-sex-sex simply oozing from both partners. Many hoped that the reported romances were true, and that King Elvis had finally found his queen. This movie was politely received although his next epic was slammed from all quarters.

Two Elvises for the price of one was the pre-publicity claim for a film Elvis was next to make for MGM. Made on a shoe-string, the budget of half a million dollars was little more than the average cost of a filmed tele-play. Consequently the finished article appeared very rough and ready. Slip-shod editing revealed a full-frontal Lance LeGault when one should have only seen his rear-end at the time he was doubling for Elvis. Still, despite the knocks, and the additional costs, when it reached the cinema in time for the Easter school holidays, it paid for itself in a week. Not bad going when you consider that it only took a mere 16 days to film. 'I had a letter recently suggesting that I should get drunk or do something different in my movies, but the type I'm making now are doing so well that it would be silly to change the formula. I've had intellectuals tell me that I've got to progress as an actor, explore new horizons, take on new challenges – all that routine. I'd like to progress, but I'm smart enough to realise that you can bite off more than you can chew in this racket. You can't go beyond your limitations. They want me to try an artistic picture – fine – maybe I can pull it off someday. But not yet. I've done eleven pictures and they've all made money. A certain type of audience likes me. I entertain them with what I am doing. It would be foolish to tamper with that kind of success.' Although Elvis scored four international chart entries throughout 1963, only one, 'Devil In Disguise', recorded at the Nashville session in April got anywhere near the top.

Still if the writing appeared to be 'on the wall' for Elvis it didn't bother him any, and at home over Christmas he made his usual donations to charity with the minimum of fuss. So pleased were the recipients that on this occasion they all clubbed together and sent Elvis a six feet square 'thank-you' card. Elvis joked that he'd have to build an extra room on to Graceland to accommodate the plaque. A local Memphis fan club joined in with mayor-making electioneering, on the promise that if the candidate was successful something in the city would be named after Elvis Presley, and the singer proudly showed everyone his new 1964 Rolls Royce.

In February 1964 Elvis kicked off his working year in the usual way by going to Hollywood to make the first of three movies. 'Roustabout', originally thought to be a skit on Colonel Parker's life story, was filmed on location at Hidden Valley, California. It was the usual pot-pourri of songs, girls, and fights, and at the end of it all Elvis caught a virus and was confined to bed. In his favour, however, he did leave his sick room to drive downtown to meet for the second time Albert Hand, who noted that the star appeared pale and tired. They talked about the Beatles and he enthused about their two television specials. 'I think the Beatles write very good songs, and I hope they don't dry-up inspiration-wise. I like "This Boy" especially, but "I Saw Her Standing There" is my personal favourite.' Hand also conversed with the Colonel's assistant Tom Diskin, who disappointed overseas audiences with a statement that Elvis would not be making any world tour!

For once Elvis didn't return to Memphis between film breaks, and preferred to entertain a few close friends at his Beverley Hills home, before going to MGM. Again Elvis was given a low-budget movie 'Girl Happy', produced by Joe Pasternak the father of an up and coming European radio giant Mike Pasternak, who broadcast in England as 'Emperor Rosko', and in France as 'Le President Rosko.'

When Elvis was finally able to return to Memphis in late summer, he had been away from Graceland for eight months. During his absence he had been elected Honorary Sheriff of Shelby County in Tennessee, and he proudly accepted the citation upon his homecoming. For $50,000 he purchased

Roosevelt's yacht, the 'Potomac' which he promptly donated to various children's charities in Tennessee, California, and Nebraska. When he presented the vessel to Danny Thomas who accepted the gift on behalf of St Jude's Hospital in Memphis, Elvis again spoke of the Beatles. 'I saw the group on the Ed Sullivan Show. I wish them all the best of luck. I don't consider the Beatles competition, just fellow artistes helping along the record industry.' A few weeks later Elvis was able to speak to Paul McCartney on the telephone. Later Paul was heard to comment that Elvis appeared 'just like one of the boys', and that he looked forward to meeting the King. He also told the Beatle that he was learning to play bass guitar (Paul's instrument) and that in doing so he ended up with very calloused hands.

Towards the end of the year Elvis returned to Hollywood, and made 'Tickle Me' for Allied Artists – as a gesture of 'goodwill'. It was known that the company was in financial difficulties and Elvis and the Colonel had stepped in to produce at least one movie on which the company could possibly hope to survive for at least a few more months. It's not reported though whether on this occasion the Colonel waived Elvis' fee, though more likely the Presley management possibly agreed to a 'pay us when you can' formula. It is known that the duo put some of their own cash into the production, and to save on expenses, old Elvis recordings, culled from LP's such as 'Pot Luck', were the backbone of the musical soundtrack. In consquence, no album (except in New Zealand) was issued bearing the movie's logo.

In 1965 Elvis celebrated his 30th birthday, and on American television veteran British pop show producer Jack Good paid tribute to Elvis on his new networking 'Shindig'. Meanwhile, in Britain several hundred fans gathered in London to attend the inauguration of the International Elvis Presley Appreciation Society. Conceived by Albert Hand, the function introduced the audience to the society's chairman Peter Aldersley – a commercial radio DJ of merit amongst the Elvis fan fraternity; and zany Jimmy Savile who had not only met Elvis in 1960, but again more recently on the Hollywood set of 'Viva Las Vegas'. A young British singer, Dave Kaye had made an anniversary tribute record 'In My Way', which was launched at the convention, having earlier been recorded by the legendary Joe Meek. Meanwhile, in the States Elvis began work on possibly his two worst ever movies – 'Harem Holiday' for MGM and 'Frankie & Johnny' at United Artists. Still, it was revealed at the time that Elvis received a cool million for each and 50% of the take. Generously Elvis made the biggest single donation to the movie industry's 'Relief Fund', some fifty thousand dollars, and then returned to Memphis and promptly purchased nine motor cycles.

In the summer the British press was filled with reports of a home-spun star Suzanna Leigh, and her forthcoming part in Presley's new movie 'Paradise Hawaiian Style'. Being made by Hal Wallis for Paramount everyone hoped against hope that he would capture some of his 'Blue Hawaii' magic, which by this time was drastically needed if the new movie was to avoid criticism.

Location shots were done over various Hawaiian Islands, although Elvis based himself on Oahu. 'I don't have to stay in my hotel room, but when fellas gather round, it's safer.' On Waikiki he occupied room 2225 on the 22nd floor of the new Illikai Hotel which is the one you see behind Jack Lord during the opening credits of the TV series 'Hawaii Five – O'. On Sunday August 15th Elvis and his party visited the Arizona Memorial commemorating the Pearl Harbour war-dead, paid for by his '61 Hawaii charity show. 'This is good. The design is so simple. I'm glad it's not gaudy – it gives me a warm feeling. It's wonderful to get a chance in your lifetime to do something of this nature. In contrast to entertaining, an opportunity such as this is especially satisfying.'

Herman's Hermits, the British craze of the time met Elvis on location at the Polynesian Cultural Centre at Laie, and Suzanna Leigh taught Elvis some British slang, 'Gor Blimey' being his favourite. Of Suzanna, Elvis commented, 'She's causing quite a stir here. She's bubbling with personality, and she's certainly the most popular girl on the film set.' Before the film crew left the island, the dancers and guides at the Cultural Centre threw a farewell party at which Elvis heard for the first time the Kui Lee song 'I'll Remember You', a local hit for

Hawaiian night club star Don Ho. Elvis pledged to record the song as soon as he could.

Filming continued on sound stage 5 at Paramount-Hollywood, and on the occasion when Elvis was perched in a heli copter he met another refugee from Great Britain – Tom Jones. At the time Jones had still to conquer the US market, though it was possibly Jones' meteoric rise to fame two years later which convinced Elvis that he had to return to live entertainment. Several of the dogs in the helicopter film sequence belonged to Elvis, including his collie 'Baba'. The film crew had to dance and jump about in an effort to entice the dogs to do the same, which made it impossible for Elvis to act his part.

On the evening of August 27th Elvis played host to the Beatles. The so-called pop summit was an event jointly arranged by a British and an American magazine. The 'party' began at 10 pm and continued through until 2.00 am when the 'fab four' left to the sounds of 'Softly As I Leave You', a track dedicated to them by Presley. Although no photographers were allowed we do know that a jam-session took place and much talk centred around Great Britain. 'Of course I would like to come to Britain! But to make a personal appearance in England would mean I should have to start a world tour, so as not to upset the other countries. I'm keenly aware of all your awards – when I win it's like a token of confidence and support. I've great respect for my British fans, but I'm sure they understand that I haven't even made a personal appearance in the States for more than four years! Don't get me wrong – I keep up with all the fan clubs, and read their newsletters. I really do care about my fans, and I love them all.'

Back on set the next day everyone wanted to know about the Beatles. 'They are fantastic guys. They are just as zany as I always imagined they would be!' When Elvis finished work on 'Paradise Hawaiian Style' he threw the usual thank you party, and handed each contributor a customary gift. This time it was a copy of his sacred album 'His Hand in Mine', and an Hawaiian flower luau. Much to his credit Elvis Presley had never forsaken his beliefs. In the early '60s he would often stop at a Los Angeles church on his way to the studios to say a silent prayer. 'I also collect Bibles. I have one in every room of my home in Memphis, and in California.'

When Elvis arrived home in the autumn he was greeted with the sad news that his old bassist friend Bill Black had died in the Memphis Baptist Hospital. He had apparently undergone surgery in the summer but died of a brain tumour at the age of 39 on October 22nd. Chart-wise the year was pretty bleak, with the exception of 'Crying in the Chapel' which surprised everyone by topping the hit parades in several countries.

And so the saga continued. The new year festivities, which included a Roman candle fight in the grounds of Graceland, Elvis enjoyed in the company of his 'inmates'. He went to Hollywood to make 'Spinout' for MGM, and returned to Memphis twelve weeks later. He bought himself another car, a black Cadillac Eldorado, and gifted his Memphis Fan Club secretary with a Chevrolet Impala. Priscilla was often seen in his company, but both were quick to squash any engagement rumours. The Presleys were so keen to deny such stories that his father Vernon wrote personally to the British music press, and Elvis Monthly. At last Elvis returned to Nashville for a session lasting for nine days, which produced all the tracking for his second sacred album 'How Great Thou Art', and the hit single 'Love Letters'.

By June 26th Elvis was on his way back to Hollywood, accompanied by Charles Hodge, a more frequent companion. They made the journey by plane, and his other 'buddies' went ahead of them, driving the required cars and a trailer-load of motorbikes. Yet another British co-star was to join Elvis in the cast of MGM's 'Double Trouble', an exceptionally pretty girl called Annette Day. On one occasion he greeted the new recruit sporting a revolting rubber vulture on his arm, with the words, 'Hi, how do you like my pet?' When she turned around to see what it was, she was horrified! On another day, Elvis prevented her from walking on set when her cue came up, by holding the back of her dress. Though location shots for this movie were filmed in Belgium, Elvis remained in Hollywood. As such filming had coincided nicely with a Brussels fan clubs' function this angered the Belgian fans, as too did the script's ridicule of the Belgian Police Force.

In October Elvis concluded his contract with Paramount by making his last movie for the studio – 'Easy Come, Easy Go'. His association with executive producer Hal Wallis had lasted for ten years, yet the plot for this feature was so trite that it bore no resemblance to his early masterpieces, 'Loving You' and 'King Creole'. When Elvis returned to Graceland in December he was pleased to see that redecorations had been executed precisely to his instructions. The master bedroom now boasted a colour TV installed in the ceiling. Another Graceland opulence for the festive season included an illuminated nativity scene in the grounds – a staff endearment which particularly delighted the Lord of the Manor.

For some four months, during his winter stay in Memphis, an Australian Fan Club president had maintained a daily vigil outside the Graceland gates. She gazed through the wrought-iron guitar plucking figures and waited patiently for Elvis' car to stop as he drove it back and forth across the electronically controlled portcullis. She had made the pilgrimage from down-under to present Elvis with an award and a token gift from her members, but as the weeks passed he continued to ignore the girl. Members of the Presley household had advised the star of her purpose, but for some reason, and completely out of character, he refused to meet her. And when he upped and left for Hollywood on March 5th, without acknowledging the young lady's presence, she was heartbroken. Such was her distress that Vernon Presley arranged for her to fly to Los Angeles, and in the fairytale tradition of 'all's-well-that-ends-well' she met her hero on the set of 'Clambake' and made her presentations. Strangely Elvis told the girl that, although he had noticed her on numerous occasions, lots of fans kept up an all year round vigil at the gates, and he thought nothing of it. He also said that no member of his staff had advised him of the reason for her visit. The event raised the question of just how much information, on all counts, was being held back from Elvis.

'Clambake' although for United Artists, was actually filmed in Universal City at the mammoth Universal Studio Complex. Elvis enjoyed making the picture, and on one glee-spree he and his friends climbed into the rafters of the preserved movie set of 'Phantom of the Opera'. A water balloon and shaving cream battle followed. On another occasion Red West staggered into view covered in studio 'blood'. Elvis was on-camera at the time, but he couldn't continue, and dissolved into fits of laughter. 'We also went on location – to a children's playground in Los Angeles city – to film a number called "Confidence". We used the kids to do the song with me, and my buddy Red West is in this scene, acting the part of an ice-cream man.'

Filming finished on Thursday, April 27th, and four days later Elvis married Priscilla Beaulieu.

CHAPTER EIGHT

'Priscilla was one of the few girls who was interested
in me, for me alone. We never discussed marriage in
Germany, we just met at her father's house, went
to the movies and did a lot of driving – that's all. I
waited for her to grow up.'

On May 1st, 1967 the World's Greatest Heart-throb married.
Well it had to happen one day, and Elvis had left it late
enough to avoid the previously predicted mass-suicides from
his legions of broken-hearted female followers. In fact his
devotees took it very well, and thousands of dollars' worth of
gifts from the singer's disciples descended upon the Presley
household. The function was stage-managed by Colonel
Parker, who arranged for the hundred or so specially invited
guests to be assembled at the reception without prior know-
ledge of what was about to happen. In the early hours a
couple of private planes arrived in Las Vegas, and the passengers were taken to the Alladin Hotel. Elvis and Priscilla collected their $15 marriage licence from the Clark County
Courthouse, and at 9.41 am the couple were married by Judge
David Zenoff. The ceremony took place in one of the hotel's
private apartments. Joe Esposito was best man, and Priscilla
was attended by her younger sister, Michelle. The wedding
breakfast was filmed for cinema newsreel, though surprisingly
the press conference which followed wasn't recorded by RCA
and subsequently released as an E.P.

'We decided to get married about six months ago, and
though we might appear calm, we certainly aren't. How can
you look happy when you're scared? We shall continue to live
in Memphis, and we hope to spend a lot of time on my new
horse farm in Mississippi.' Elvis had decided to invest in
blood-stock and to that end he had acquired a sizeable 163-acre
ranch near Walls, just across the Tennessee state line. It was

later to be christened 'The Circle G'.

Festivities over, the happy couple honeymooned in Palm Springs, interrupted for final dubbing on 'Clambake' at Universal, and then on May 4th retreated to the comparative privacy of Graceland. The Presleys relaxed, went riding, drove around in Elvis' new cream-coloured Eldorado, and practised yoga. On 29th, they threw a mini-reception for those friends who through secrecy were unable to attend the Las Vegas ceremony, and shared part of the six-tiered cake salvaged from the Alladin.

But on June 19th it was back to work, after driving Priscilla from Memphis to Hollywood. Elvis reported to MGM to commence work on 'Speedway', and Priscilla took on the house-wife role at Palm Springs.

'I'm the happiest person in the world!' Elvis exclaimed to his equally famous co-star Nancy Sinatra on the 'Speedway' set. 'I've known Nancy since we did her dad's 'Welcome Home Elvis' TV show. Ever since then we've been running into each other. It was a great thing for us to work together!' Working together, though, wasn't that easy. Love scenes were sabotaged, with the couple erupting into fits of giggles, which was to annoy the director so much that he sent them both home for the day. Norman Taurog had to tolerate further Presley pranks, which included locking up Miss Sinatra so that she never made it on time when the director called her on set, and frequent pillow fights. At the end of the filming Elvis gifted Nancy with an electric golf caddy and filled her dressing room with flowers to overflowing. The cast also threw a party for Elvis, and this time it was to celebrate the announcement that Priscilla and Elvis were expecting a baby. Elvis had never been seen to be so happy. He was whistling and singing all day.

When 'Speedway' was completed the couple spent a further two days in Las Vegas before returning to Memphis to be greeted by a mountain of packages, each one earmarked for the new arrival. Elvis added a further two cars to his fleet and bought several bicycles. Although in the eyes of the press the Presleys were good news in 1967, little had been happening for the star with respect to chart placings, or film appeal. This was all to change when on September 10th Elvis attended a three-day recording session in Nashville and taped 'Big Boss Man' and 'Guitar Man'. At last the singer was beginning to see the light again.

The Governor of Tennessee proclaimed September 29th 'Elvis Presley Day', and Elvis was well pleased! 'I just don't know what to say! Just tell everyone I love 'em, and thank 'em. I hope I can live up to this great honour Governor Ellington has bestowed on me. It's really nice.' Earlier in the year Major Ingram had jumped the gun somewhat by announcing that the newly constructed Mid-South Coliseum was to be re-named 'The Elvis Presley Coliseum', though when he flunked re-election the plans were dropped.

In the autumn Elvis flew to Culver City to start work on 'Stay Away, Joe', a movie which, according to Tom Diskin (Colonel Parker's P.A.) was to offer the star a new acting challenge. 'I'd like to prove myself as an actor, but I'm still not sure of my ability. Right now I'm still taking little steps in that direction. I look at my old movies and I can pick up on my mistakes. There's a lot I'd like to change. In "Stay Away, Joe" I'm a wheeler-dealer who's always promoting something. It's a more grown-up character – part Hud, part Alfie. He's always looking out for women, but not wanting them to chase him. In this film I only do three songs, and I get the opportunity to do a lot more acting.' Location shots for the movie were filmed in Sedona, Arizona.

When Elvis and Priscilla returned to Memphis for Christmas they were welcomed by the usual pile of gifts, plus the ever-growing second pile of toys and clothing for the new baby, which was due to arrive in the early part of 1968.

The New Year was to be the turning point in Elvis' career that all his fans had anxiously hoped for. The tracks he'd cut in Nashville a few months earlier were now firmly entrenched in the international hit parades and Elvis was about to reject the seclusion of the movie industry. During the previous years Elvis Presley had only worked for 100 days out of 365, and the reasons for the lack of live appearances were confused. With only a third of his working year occupied, there was always time to accommodate additional activities, and the excuses given to prevent this were often feeble. 1968 was, for Elvis, the year of changes.

In January Colonel Parker stunned everyone by announcing that NBC was to finance Elvis' return to television, and there was more to come!!! On February 1st Elvis hurried his wife to the Memphis Baptist Hospital and at 5.01 pm on the same day Priscilla gave birth to their baby daughter. She weighed 6 lbs 15 ozs and the following day it was announced that she was to be named 'Lisa Marie'. Was it coincidence that the Colonel's wife's name is Marie? (Had the baby been male it was to be named John Barron) Elvis beamed! 'Oh man, she's just too much! I'm still a little shaky. She's a doll. What can you do, but just sit there holding her, and then you say to yourself, "Hey – that's my kid!" She's great! Everyone seems to like the name Lisa Marie. I felt all along she'd be a girl, and I was secretly sorta hoping for a daughter. I can just see myself about sixteen years from now, checking out all the fellas who want to date her!'

At the end of the month Elvis returned to California, to be followed a few days later by Priscilla and their baby. Elvis' father Vernon drove to Los Angeles to ferry over Elvis' new Mark III Lincoln Continental only to find that he was to be used as an extra in the new Presley movie 'Live a Little Love a Little', loosely based on the novel 'Kiss My Firm, but Pliant Lips', being made by MGM. Locations for the film included 'Marineland of the Pacific', the Los Angeles Music Centre, and the superb California coastline, but it was never screened in British cinemas. 'I'm still trying to change my image, and make better movies.'

On the weekend of April 6th/7th Elvis and Priscilla drove some 300 miles to Las Vegas. It was a journey which was to give Elvis the taste again for live entertainment, having led a standing ovation at the Midnight Tom Jones show at the Flamingo Hotel. Backstage they renewed their acquaintance, and Elvis told the British star how moved he and his friends were when they heard Tom's recording of 'Green Green Grass of Home'. 'I liked your recording of *Delilah*. Priscilla is a big Tom Jones' fan, but I told her to cool-it tonight. When "Green Green Grass of Home" was released the boys and I were driving home in our big bus. That disc meant so much to us boys from Memphis that we just sat there and cried. Later we called the radio station and they played it for us four more times.'

Elvis and Tom also discussed diets, and Elvis quipped that he, too, was watching his weight again. 'I'm on what they call a drinking man's diet. I put it on across the cheeks!'

When he returned to Los Angeles he told Colonel Parker about the show, and the Colonel said that he would begin to 'look-around' at the market. 'Live a Little' over, the couple and baby Lisa flew to Hawaii for a belated first wedding anniversary treat. The trio took a boat trip out to see the Arizona Memorial, and as it was Priscilla's first visit to the Islands Elvis spoke proudly of the concert he performed in 1961 which contributed to the building of the monument. He also revealed that he was excitingly awaiting his forthcoming television show.

Relaxed and tanned Elvis returned to Los Angeles and headed for 'beautiful downtown Burbank' to commence rehearsals for his NBC special. For two weeks Elvis, the dancers, and his musicians began putting their routines together, and on Thursday, June 27th the first segment was taped. Two hundred fans filled the tiny studio; each one perching on a series of tiered seats arranged around three sides of a 15-foot-square stage. Four different sessions were recorded and twenty-five different numbers were performed, including 'Tip Toe Through the Tulips' à la Tiny Tim, and 'MacArthur Park', but sadly the majority was to end up on the cutting-room floor. Elvis had done it, and watched by Priscilla, who attended one of the sessions, he proved that he could still perform alongside the best of them! 'If I Can Dream', the concluding number in the programme, was heralded as one of the most socially aware performances of our time.

Everyone then had to wait until December 3rd, the planned transmission date for the programme, which was sponsored by The Singer Corporation – the sewing machine giant. In the meantime Elvis spoke about the show. 'I hope it'll be full of surprises. I missed making PAs, so perhaps there is hope for that in 1969. I figured it was about time – I thought that I'd better do it before I get too old. When I started all my fans were teenagers, now they're all mothers and fathers. I realise that I couldn't go on doing the same things, and from now on I hope I don't have to make so many movies. There's been a great change in music – the sounds have changed – the musicians have changed, but I haven't changed much really. For the show I've chosen the music carefully, and we've improved the sounds. I never realised that I missed live performances so much until recently. When I get back on the road I'll probably start out in this country, but I intend to play abroad, starting with Europe. I want to see places I've never seen before. Except for movies and albums, it's been a long time since I've done anything professionally!'

Elvis had admitted that the return to TV had taken a lot out of him. He was very nervous, and had lost several nights' sleep before the actual recordings. So he needed ten days to relax in his Palm Springs residence before driving to Apache Junction in Arizona (about thirty miles from Phoenix) to film location shots for 'Charro', a movie made for National General, but filmed by MGM camera crew. For his part Elvis had to grow a beard, and to compete with him, so did Colonel Parker and Joe Esposito. Elvis' co-star in the production was Linn Kellogg, the Broadway star of the musical 'Hair'. Off-set she would often duet with Elvis while Charlie Hodge played guitar. 'This is the first movie I've ever made without singing a song. I play a gunfighter and to be honest, we couldn't see a singing gunfighter.' Back in Culver City Elvis boasted daily about his daughter, 'I wouldn't change anything in my private life right now. That little girl of mine is really something. I look forward to seeing her every night after work. Things in general are looking good. Even rock 'n' roll is going strong again – a lot of people are singing it now. I'm looking forward to live appearances, and that TV show has gotten me in the mood for appearances again. I've got just two movies for MGM and one for Universal, then off we go ...'

Elvis returned to Memphis on September 25th, and his return to Graceland was more eagerly awaited than at any time before. Friends, fans, and relatives were anxious to see how Lisa had grown up during the seven months they had been away. But it was a vacation marked by sadness, as the DJ who gave Elvis his start died in a Memphis hospital. 'I'm awfully hurt and feel dreadfully upset about hearing of Dewey's death. We were such good friends, and I never forgot the things he did for me. He launched my career in those early days.' 1968 also witnessed the passing of Steve Sholes, the RCA A & R man who signed Elvis to the company. In October Elvis returned to Hollywood to make his final scripted movie for MGM, originally titled 'Chatauqua!', but subsequently released as 'The Trouble with Girls (or how to get into it)'. It's no secret that the tame script angered Elvis, 'I would like to get away from musicals, and films like this. If only I could get my hands on a good, serious dramatic part! I don't have the privilege of script approval I'm afraid. The problem is, they keep trying to make 'GI Blues' and 'Blue Hawaii' over and over again, and all they do is move the scenery around a little.' During the night filming the temperature lowered to such an extent that Elvis' jaw froze and he couldn't speak, but as usual he amused the cast and crew during breaks. Off set he would pick up his guitar and sing 'By the Time I get to Phoenix' and 'MacArthur Park', and like everyone else he rejoiced when the press acclaimed his TV show after it was first seen in the United States on December 3rd.

Colonel Parker had made sure that the NBC Television Special would generate its own publicity, and with the Colonel's own publicity machine in action the effect was outstanding. Radio Stations heralded the news of the forthcoming special, and RCA was busily getting copies of the TV Show's soundtrack (Elvis' first ever 'live' album) into the shops. The Singer Company were also privileged by being able to exclusively retail through stores, a budget-priced album of Presley tracks later to be re-issued by RCA Camden. Fan clubs in other parts of the world were busy petitioning TV stations for the Elvis Presley NBC Special to be shown in their country, and in Britain this was no exception. The British fan club, which a year earlier had been 'acquired' by the writer, showered the BBC with thousands of requests for the special programme, and at the club's annual convention in July the topic on everyone's lips was the TV show. However the 2,000 strong audience were able to enjoy a premier screening of 'Speedway', arranged by Colonel Parker, with an on-screen message written by Elvis preceding the presentation, plus a

70

rare viewing of 'King Creole' by courtesy of Hal Wallis. Conventions of this kind are staged annually all around the world, but none of them as exciting as the programmes arranged by the British Fan Club. On this occasion Emperor Rosko, the son of Presley film producer Joe Pasternak guested along with Radio Luxembourg DJ Tony Prince.

In Australia, RCA arranged for Elvis' gold Cadillac to go on tour, on behalf of several charities, and in the same year Elvis auctioned his 1964 Rolls Royce and handed over the proceeds to a Memphis charity.

After 'The Trouble with Girls' had been completed Elvis returned to Memphis for a typical 'Graceland Christmas'. Vernon Presley dressed up as Santa Claus, which delighted the eleven-month-old Lisa who was almost walking by now.

Early in 1969 Elvis made an unprecedented move. He decided to cut an album at the American Recording Studios, on Danny Thomas Boulevard, in Memphis. Never before had he worked outside the RCA–Movie Industry umbrella, but he began a session which was to re-establish the star in the eyes of his critics. It was reported that almost seventy songs were recorded, and during the session (which Elvis had to interrupt because of a mild attack of tonsillitis) every session man worth his salt had to fight hard to keep up with the singer. 'As far as I am concerned, Memphis is the place. I can do sessions at home, without having to travel to other parts of the country – and the musicians here – they are fantastic, man; just fantastic!'

Pleased with the sessions, Elvis flew to a ski-lodge in Aspen, Colorado, with Priscilla and Lisa, and there they celebrated the girl's first birthday.

By now word was already reaching the press that Elvis was to appear at a session of concerts in Las Vegas, though for many months the information was very sketchy. In the meantime, in early March, Elvis returned to LA to commence work on 'Change of Habit' at Universal City. Filming was mostly centred in and around Universal's famous 'New York Street' backlot, used constantly for TV productions such as 'Kojak'. The studio operate guided tours around their empire everyday in vehicles known as 'glamor-trams', and at least one lucky group got to meet Elvis on one of the sound-stages and obtain his treasured autograph. Gospel singer Mahalia Jackson also visited the star at Universal.

' "Change of Habit" is a change of pace for me. It's more serious than my usual movies, though there are no real dramatic scenes. I wanted to try something different, and I chose this film because the script is a good one. I've just made "Charro" which apart from the title song has no singing scenes, and this movie will only have a couple. I play the part of a doctor, which is nice – I remember as a kid I always wanted to go into medicine, and I still read a few books on the subject. I think there's one song in this film you'll like – it's called "Rubberneckin'". It's a difficult number to pick guitar to, and my fingers are getting all ripped up from playing in rehearsals. Although I'm not planning too far ahead, you've possibly heard that a session of live shows in Las Vegas is on the cards. I'm looking forward to that, followed by perhaps another movie, and then I hope to honour my obligations to my fans in Europe – I know I keep promising, but this time I hope we can do something about it! I won't start to think about my stage act, or what I'm going to wear until I finish "Change of Habit". There will be plenty of time to plan it carefully. I'll be a little nervous, and for the first two or three nights I'll get butterflies, but hopefully I'll be able to take it in my stride.'

When the couple flew off to Hawaii at the end of filming, divorce rumours were already beginning to make the headlines. But on the Islands the couple seemed happy enough, enjoying the sea, the sun, and one of Tom Jones' shows at a leading hotel. In May Elvis and Priscilla returned to Memphis, but not before making a historic journey to the State of Nevada.

Hotelier Kirk Kerkorian flew Elvis to Las Vegas in his private DC-9 to the partly completed sight of his new 'International Hotel'. Within its massive complex there was a luxurious 2,000 seater theatre, and on its stage Elvis was to perform for a fee of $150,000 a week.

Barbara Streisand opened the hotel with a four-week season on July 3rd, but by now all interest had centred upon Elvis' arrival in the town one month later. Already the showroom was booked to overflowing, and even before setting foot on the International's stage Elvis had broken all-time Las Vegas showroom attendance records.

Elvis had meanwhile decided to sell his ranch, moving his horses to the Graceland estate. Each day Priscilla and husband would exercise their animals, much to the delight of the onlookers. At one time it was reported that the couple were signing some autographs for two to three hours each day in temperatures of 100° F. It the middle of June Elvis had been fitted out with his new costumes, so by July 5th he was ready to leave Memphis for the West Coast. Elvis had already chosen his backing band, and the musicians assembled for rehearsals in Los Angeles. James Burton (Lead Guitar), John Wilkinson (Rhythm Guitar), Ronnie Tutt (Drums), Jerry Scheff (Bass Guitar), Larry Muhoberac (Piano), and Charlie Hodge (Guitar/Vocals/'Factotum') were the chosen few.

'In the Ghetto' was an international number one hit, and the star was poised to launch into orbit.

CHAPTER NINE

On July 21st, 1969, man stepped on to the moon; the eagle had landed and Neil Armstrong made one small step for man, and one giant step for mankind. The world's attention focused on Tranquillity Base, and history was made. On July 31st, 1969 Elvis Presley stepped on to the 'International' stage – the King had returned. It might have been one small step for Elvis – but it was a giant step for his fans (Elvis Monthly – Great Britain, written by researcher Anne Nixon)

Petula Clark, Ann-Margret, George Hamilton IV, Wayne Newton, Shirley Bassey, Pat Boone, Dick Clark, and Angie Dickenson were amongst the dozens of showbusiness personalities who joined a 2,000 strong audience to greet Elvis on his return to live entertainment. The group played a driving riff, and almost by surprise Elvis exploded on to the stage. He was wearing a black two-piece karate style suite (a forerunner of his trend-setting jump-suit to be latched on to by Neil Diamond, The Osmonds, and the like) completed with a sash. An Apache scarf untidily hung around his neck, and the artiste was lean and trim. His neatly arranged hair collapsed, framing his face as he launched into 'Blue Suede Shoes' accompanying himself on a guitar borrowed from Charlie Hodge. His animated form gyrated across the huge stage, and he took care to share his new found nearness with every member of the audience. The first concert was used as a platform to introduce his new blockbuster single 'Suspicious Minds', which was vocally supported by the four-girl group, the Sweet Inspirations, and the male quartet The Imperials. Bobby Morris conducted the showroom orchestra. Elvis concluded his act with 'What'd I Say' and walked off stage to a standing ovation. Triumphantly Elvis returned on stage to encore and closed with 'Can't Help

Falling in Love'. Even his most severe critics, hoping and expecting the worst, mellowed, but proudest of all that first night was pretty Priscilla.

After the show the press applauded Elvis as he joined them in one of the hotel's private conference suites for a press reception. 'We had to complete our movie contracts before we could start on live appearances, but here I am. And I'll be the first to admit that I've missed all this live contact with an audience. It was getting harder and harder to sing to a camera all day long. Let's face it, when you have ten different songs for each new movie, they can't all be good. Eventually I got tired of singing to turtles, and guys who I'd just beaten up. I chose to open in Las Vegas as this is an international town, and folks travel here from all over. Tonight – our opening night – was just the most exciting time of my life. I was nervous for the first three numbers, but after that I began to loosen up ... one day I'll fall apart. I've chosen a Negro-girl back-up group because they help to give me my feel – my soul. "In the Ghetto" re-started it all – it was such a great song, I really couldn't pass it up. But there'll be no more leather jackets for me. When I did my recent TV special I roasted in it under those lights. I've chosen to wear this two-piece suit on stage as it keeps me cool, and I got the idea for it from a karate outfit I once had. Now I've returned to the scene I realise now I have something to work for, and with Lisa and Priscilla who have both changed my life – I have something to live for. Sometimes when I get home and see all those gold discs on the wall, I never connect them as belonging to me.'

Elvis entertained twice nightly from then on for his almost month-long season. Jerry Lee Lewis, Tom Jones, Shelley Fabares, Nancy Sinatra, and other artists helped to swell the attendance figures at each concert. Elvis alternated his clothing and routines to ensure that most shows were anchored to a different format and the most popular repertoire for the season included 'Hound Dog', 'All Shook Up', 'In the Ghetto', 'Mystery Train', 'Tiger Man', 'Are You Lonesome Tonight', 'Memories', 'Words', 'I Can't Stop Loving You', 'Johnny B. Goode', 'Runaway', 'My Babe', 'Hey Jude', 'Yesterday', 'Loving You', and 'Money Honey'.

On August 21st, for the final week of the engagement RCA's Felton Jarvis arrived to supervise recordings of his act for a future second live album. After the final curtain Elvis remained in the hotel to 'party' and to attend the opening of Nancy Sinatra's follow-up season.

Satisfied with his efforts, Elvis relaxed in the privacy of his Bel-Air and Palm Springs homes before returning to Memphis on September 23rd. Elvis' fans rejoiced at the success, but none so passionately as the 2,000 plus who attended a British Fan Club Convention on September 21st. They were treated to a premiere of the hitherto unseen NBC Elvis TV Special, which was subsequently purchased by the BBC for end-of-the-year screening. BBC Television recorded highlights of the fan gathering for one of their news programmes, and on this occasion Rosko, Tony Prince, and the writer were joined by Jimmy Savile and British singing star Anita Harris who headed an impressive guest list that attracted such a huge crowd which in turn raised over £1,000 for a Guide Dog charity.

In October Elvis took Priscilla to Hawaii, and then on to a private Nassau estate in the Bahamas for a holiday, staying away from his Memphis home whilst re-decoration was in progress. But it was all completed in time for the usual Christmas festivities, and the Presleys old and young were united again for their Yuletide in Memphis. December sales of 'Suspicious Minds' earned Elvis another 'gold record award.'

1970 started off with more impending divorce rumours, and whilst there were still no comments from Elvis about the allegations, some reports were beginning to sound credible. Six days into the New Year Elvis flew to Los Angeles to rehearse for his second Las Vegas stint which opened again in the International on Monday, January 26th. Fears that a return to the gambling mecca were too premature were dispelled, as record-breaking audiences queued for up to eight hours to ensure good seating for each performance. Juliet Prowse, George Chakiris, Zsa Zsa Gabor, and Dean Martin joined the invited guest line for the first show, and hearing that Dino was amongst the multitude, he couldn't resist singing a few bars of 'Everybody Loves Somebody Sometime' much to the star's amusement. Ronnie Tutt and Larry Muhoberac were replaced by Bob Lanning (drums) and Glenn Hardin (piano), although the rest of the line up remained the same. Comedian Sammy Shore, as for Elvis' first International season, acted as warm-up act. Lisa was now two years old, and was often seen escorted into the showroom by mummy Priscilla.

For much of the engagement Elvis had a dose of the 'flu, though this passed by virtually unnoticed, and the affliction cannot be detected on the resulting 'On Stage' album recorded by RCA during the final week.

The four-week season had earned Elvis Presley something in the region of three quarters of a million dollars, and hotel boss Kirk Kerkorian, pleased at the success, loaned Elvis the use of his executive jet to transport him to Houston where Elvis was to entertain 250,000 people. Six concerts were arranged as part of the annual Rodeo and Livestock Show staged in the town's huge Astrodome. There were two shows each day on Friday, February 27th, Saturday 28th, and Sunday, March 1st, and the matinee performance on Friday played to a crowd of school children including some 4,000 handicapped kids who were there as guests of Elvis and the Colonel. The line up for the six shows was the same as in Las Vegas, and following the concerts Elvis gave the now customary press conference held in the Astroworld Hotel.

'As you will see I'm unable to use the Jordanaires in my act, and I know that's disappointed a lot of people. The fact is, I can't get the boys out of Nashville to go on the road with me. They're making too much money at home. I've enjoyed this visit to Texas, especially as I started out my career in this area. I got a big thrill out of working the " 'Dome". I knew it would be hard, as it's difficult to get any personal contact with such a big audience. That's why I toured the edge of the stadium in a convertible before getting on stage. I just decided to get out there and work as hard as I could, and get off quickly. I'm pleased with what's happening now – I can do what I feel. I can't even bear to watch re-runs of my old movies on TV any more, so if we make more films in the future the scripts will have to be updated. I'm getting too critical, and perhaps that's a good thing. Besides, the sound and everything has changed now – I think, for the better.' After the reception Elvis was presented with five gold awards, and the following afternoon Mr and Mrs Presley returned to Beverley Hills, then on to Palm Springs for a vacation.

During the months to come the singer's routine was unchanged. In May he signed a three-movie contract with MGM, and the following month Elvis went to Nashville for several weekend all-through-the-night recording sessions. James Burton was now to join Elvis on most of these, bringing a richer quality to an ever-increasingly commercial product which was to maintain Elvis' continued high chart positions in future years.

In July Elvis was back at MGM, working on the first film of his new contract. But it wasn't the usual movie – in fact it was a documentary of the 'new style' Elvis – Elvis in concert. Director Dennis Sanders filmed Elvis in rehearsal and in the MGM sound stage studios. Local fans in the California area were interviewed, and when Elvis returned to Las Vegas to fulfil his summer contract with the International Hotel the camera team were in there punching with Elvis for the first show.

'This is the nitty gritty time, as far as being nervous, you know – opening night, man. You should have seen me at dinner tonight, when I was going in tempo (to the music). I never swallowed any of it. If the songs don't go over, we can do a medley of costumes.' By now Elvis had geared his stage wear to the jumpsuit, obtaining a stunning new collection from the hands of designer Bill Belew. First-night guest stars included Sammy Davis Jnr., Cary Grant, Juliet Prowse, Sonny Liston, Jack Benny, Nancy Sinatra, and Mr and Mrs Xavier Cugat. Each was given a bag of goodies, which included a polystyrene 'straw' boater, sported by most members of the audience that season. Casino croupiers, bar staff, and management alike all had to wear the hats, upon the instructions of Colonel Parker. The line up enjoyed the return of ace drummer Ronnie Tutt, and this time Joe Guercio conducted the showroom orchestra. High female vocals were by courtesy of Millie Kirkham, who worked out of Nashville.

Elvis was now to give back-stage audiences to specific guests. Peter Aldersley, former Radio Luxembourg DJ, and at the time an officer for RCA's UK operations met Elvis in Las Vegas and was told, 'I am coming to Europe for a tour, and I'm very much looking forward to seeing Britain and the Continent. All the plans for the tour are being discussed right now.' The message was no different to what had been told to extrovert entertainer Screaming Lord Sutch in February of the same year. 'Tom Jones asked why I don't come to England to see my real fans instead of playing Las Vegas. I can't believe I'm that popular there. I think we must now do a tour of the world's capitals.'

Almost at every meeting Elvis was quizzed about tours outside of the confines of the United States. And more often than not, a trip to Europe was emphasised as being imperative.

When Elvis closed his third Las Vegas engagement he embarked on a whistle-stop tour, his first since 1957, visiting Phoenix, Arizona on September 9th; St Louis, Missouri; Detroit, Michigan; Miami, Florida (for two shows); Tampa Florida (two shows); and on September 14th, Mobile, Alabama.

Meanwhile in Europe Elvis fans converged on the tiny principality of Luxembourg. An international convention was staged by the Official Elvis Presley Fan Club of Great Britain with the help of Radio Tele Luxembourg in association with several of the larger European based clubs. For many the occasion began a week before as a party of 300 English fans toured Belgium, Holland, Germany, and France before arriving in the Grand Duchy in time for the function on Saturday, September 5th, held in the newly constructed state-owned 'Theatre Nouveau' Dennis Sanders and a team of camera crew and technicians had flown from the States to record the event for inclusion in the new documentary movie. On stage in Luxembourg RCA's representative Peter Aldersley announced Elvis' intentions of a European tour. His revelations fell upon 'we've heard it all before' ears, and the news was greeted with the same cynicism as Elvis' reported gift to the convention audience – a bicycle made for two. The tandem was raffled off for charity, and Sanders returned with film of the exercise, the convention entertainment, and footage of of Aldersley and Radio Luxembourg DJ Tony Prince riding the bike through the Germanic streets of the city. The convention audience was able to enjoy a European première of 'Change of Habit', which was just as well, as the movie was never released on to the European cinema circuits, although it was shown on British television some years later.

Dennis Sanders arrived back in the States in time to supervise filming of Elvis' Phoenix audience reaction, which was used underneath the opening sequence credits of 'Elvis That's the Way It Is'. The title was Elvis' own choice. 'I think it's the best film I've ever made in ten years!'

After the tour, Elvis added a Stutz Blackhawk car to his collection and had it driven to Memphis. On October 13th he flew home, and attended a Gospel Quartet convention held in the city on Thursday and Saturday of the same week. At the same time he was appointed a deputy sheriff of Shelby County, which enabled him to wear a gun.

By November 10th another tour was under way – this time centred around the West Coast areas, commencing in Oakland, California, and then travelling to Portland, Oregon; Seattle, Washington State; San Francisco, California; Los Angeles, California (two shows); San Diego, California; Oklahoma City; and concluding in Denver, Colorado State, on November 17th. His concerts in Los Angeles at the Inglewood Forum will be remembered for his on-stage attack at certain gossip-riddled movie magazines. 'A lot of things are being printed about me, and most of it is untrue! Many people are led to believe that 'Hound Dog' is my biggest seller. But that's not so – it's 'Now or Never'. That single sold twenty millions. I've got fifty-six gold singles and fourteen gold albums, and if there's anyone out there who doubts it, if you ever come through Memphis, you can come in and argue about it – 'cause I've got 'em hangin' on the walls. I'm really proud of 'em. I've sold over 200 million actual records. I've outsold the Beatles and Jones, and all of 'em put together!'

Elvis and family returned to Memphis for Christmas and the New Year, and he drove across the state border into Mississippi on December 29th to pay a private visit to Tupelo to view the 'Elvis Presley Centre' and to 'see friends'.

During 1970 Elvis had a string of top twenty hits, and had returned to live entertainment, not only with Las Vegas, but now he was on the road for real. His movie 'That's the Way It Is' was playing to sell-out audiences and future tours were planned for the new year. It came as no surprise, therefore, when, on January 16th, Elvis Presley was chosen as one of the 'Ten Outstanding Men of 1970' by the Jaycees Award Committee. Elvis received his award watched by Priscilla at a ceremony staged at the Holiday Inn and The Ellis Auditorium in Memphis. 'I read books, and I was the hero of the comic book. I saw movies, and I was the hero of the movie. So every dream that I have ever had has come true a hundred times. That's all a man can ask. These gentlemen over here, these are the type of people who care – they're dedicated! You realise that it's not impossible that they might be building the Kingdom of Heaven. It's not too far-fetched from reality. I would like to say that I learned from very early in life that without a song, the day would never end. Without a song, man ain't got a friend. Without a song, the road would never end. Without a song. So I keep singing the song!'

Also in January, Elvis was best man at colleague Sonny West's wedding, with Priscilla acting as maid-of-honour, before heading for Las Vegas for season number four commencing on January 26th. Elvis had now consolidated his stage performance, though he enhanced the general format with the inclusion of several new songs. This season they were 'Get Back', 'Something', 'Help Me Make it through the Night', and the showstopper 'How Great Thou Art'. The International Hotel presented Elvis with a $10,000 solid gold attendance record award belt buckle which he proudly wore on stage. But the season wasn't all that happy for the King of Las Vegas. He was plagued with the 'flu, requiring the continual attendance of a doctor in the wings which he had to endure along with several death threats. The latter precipitated investigation by the FBI, and armed guards positioned themselves just off the showroom stage. At the end of the season Elvis gifted the follow-up act, Ann-Margret, with a 6-foot floral guitar, and the star and wife sat ringside for the opening concert.

A quick visit to Palm Springs preceded the usual return to

Memphis and a recording session in Nashville commenced on March 15th. After a day, however, Elvis was driven to hospital suffering from an eye infection, and he later flew to Hawaii to recuperate – more food for the movie magazines, who decided that Elvis was now going blind. When he returned to Memphis in April, Elvis was seen to be wearing a black eye patch. The Nashville session was resumed in May, and more recording was done in June. Also in June it was announced that a 12-mile stretch of highway which runs past Graceland was to have a name change. Previously known as 'Highway 51 South', – it was now designated as 'Elvis Presley Boulevard'. Elvis missed the announcement, and later he admitted to being unaware of the change, until one day he saw a television commercial in which an advertiser had listed his address as being on 'Elvis Presley Boulevard'.

Now it was time to return to the night-club scene, although this time Las Vegas wasn't the town. Elvis was booked to appear at Lake Tahoe, a picturesque lakeside gambling resort in Northern Nevada. Half the town is on the right side of the Nevada State line, where gambling and such like is permitted, and the left-hand section protrudes into the Californian state, where such goings on are prohibited. Elvis opened at the Sahara Tahoe on July 20th and played to a more intimate cabaret audience through till August 2nd. The season was a huge success, and management gifted Elvis with a diamond watch to complement his half a million dollar fee. It was no secret, however, that the staff were glad to see the back of the singer who had attracted more supporters than they had originally forecast and for the most part they were unprepared for the avalanche of fans who daily descended upon the property.

With only a week in between, Elvis returned to Las Vegas and the International Showroom. By now ownership of the luxury hotel complex had been gained by the Hilton chain. Anyone associated with Elvis was now easily spotted in the casino and lounge areas, as Elvis had given each a golden chain with a TCB pendant. The initials stand for 'Taking Care of Business' and the logo includes a lightning flash. In later months more favoured associates had this standard 'medal' replaced with a much better pendant complete with a diamond setting. Backstage Elvis received the 'Bing Crosby Award' presented to him by the NARAS on behalf of his services to the music industry. Having sold his Hillcrest Road home in LA, and in the process of moving into a more secluded property in Monovale Road, Beverly Hills, Elvis returned to Memphis when his Las Vegas season finished on September 6th.

At the end of October European fans gathered together for an international convention, the event being staged by the British Fan Club, in Paris. Elvis commenced a twelve city tour in Minneapolis on November 5th followed by Cleveland, Ohio (two shows); Louisville, Kentucky; Philadelphia, Pennsylvania; Baltimore, Maryland; Boston, Massachusetts; Cincinnati, Ohio; Huston, Texas; Dallas, Texas (two shows); Tuscaloosa, Alabama; Kansas City, Missouri; winding up in Salt Lake City, Utah on November 16th. The Imperials were replaced by J.D. Sumner and the Stamps Quartet, and comedian Jackie Kahane also now became a regular member of the Presley Circus. On the morning of the Baltimore concert Elvis visited the Narcotics Bureau in Washington, but was rejected when they turned down a $5,000 donation which he offered in exchange for a Federal Narcotics Badge. However, a meeting later in the afternoon with President Nixon in the White House secured the Narcotics Badge for Elvis' collection.

And so back to Memphis!

A New Year brought a fresh crop of new announcements. 1972 was to see the official dedication of 'Elvis Presley Boulevard', Elvis' triumphant stage act was to be presented in New York, and there was a follow-up film to 'Elvis That's the Way It Is'.

Elvis began his public year by opening his sixth Las Vegas season on January 26th. In March Elvis was back at MGM – with a band. Producing duo Pierre Adidge and Robert Abel had been awarded a Presley–Parker carte blanche to record on celluloid some of Elvis' more intimate creative moments. With unobtrusive hand-held 16 mm cameras the couple invaded his privacy, and filmed the session which subsequently evolved. When Elvis went on tour in April, so did Adidge and Abel. From Buffalo on April 5th the showed moved to Detroit, to Dayton, to Knoxville, to Hampton Roads, to Richmond, to Roanoke, to Indianapolis, to Charlotte, to Greensboro, to Macon, to Jacksonville, to Little Rock, to San Antonio, and finished in Alberquerque on April 19th. (A day earlier Albert Hand, editor of 'Elvis Monthly', died in England.) Privately, Elvis was pleased to conclude this series of appearances. It gave him the time to return to Memphis, and to take Lisa and Priscilla to Hawaii in May to attend an island karate tournament. Elvis used the time to attempt to patch up an ever-widening rift in his marriage. Both sides were eager for progress, but as the weeks passed, all reconciliation attempts failed.

Work continued. New York was buzzing in anticipation of Presley's projected concerts at Madison Square Garden, but anxious not to be swept too soon into the fever, Elvis went to Vegas to see Glen Campbell in concert.

On June 9th a press conference was staged in the Mercury Ballroom at the New York Hilton. At 4.00 pm Elvis met the press, flanked on-camera by Vernon, and off-camera by Colonel Parker. Elvis wore a blue-caped coat and a big smile, and he spoke kindly to cub reporter and media giant alike. 'First of all I plead innocent of all charges (attributed to Elvis' delay in appearing in New York City). I understand it was just a matter of getting the right building – we couldn't get a good one in fifteen years. All kiddin' aside, we had to wait our turn to get into the Garden. I just hope we put on a good show ... I've taken Vitamin E!'

It was as if the press boys had never read the transcripts of previous Presley interviews, and again the major questions centred around Elvis' audience, his movements, and his greasy hair. 'Man I stopped using that greasy kid's stuff, just like everyone did. The movements, are you kiddin'? I was tame (in the early days) compared to what they do now. I didn't do anything but jiggle! It's been hard to live up to an image, [so] I can't criticise anyone else in the entertainment field. I think that there's room for everybody. I hate to criticise another performer – the image is one thing, the human being is another. I've found that our audiences are now very mixed. It's older people too, as well as the young and very young. All types of people. I missed the closeness of live audiences, so just as soon as I got out of the movie contracts, I started to do live performances again. There are so many places I haven't been yet. I've never played New York until now. I've never been to Britain either, I'd like to go to Japan. I've never been out of this country, except for the services.'

'I don't have any aspirations in politics, or anything of that nature. I'm just an entertainer, so I'd just as soon keep my personal opinions to myself.'

'As far as movies, if you're talking about a non-singing role, yes, I'd like to do that. We're looking right now for a script, but we'll only do it if we can find the right kind of property. It's hard to find good material nowadays [and that includes new songs]. It's very difficult to find any [new, and good] hard rock songs [at this time]. If I could find them, I would do them. [There's not much point in looking back to the fifties for such material.] I'd like to think that we've improved ourselves over the past fifteen years [both] musically and vocally. I'd like to think I've improved.'

Elvis went on to explain that because songwriters found it more profitable to sing their own material, little was left available for the singer. 'Once they get a hit record, they form their own company – there's so many of them. I have my own music publishing company, but I still take songs from anywhere, or from anybody – if they're good. Even from a completely unknown.'

Saying that he wasn't ashamed of his musical roots, he continued: 'And I'm not going to retire – I've still too much energy. I'll keep going on for as long as I can. [And now] I have to get back to rehearsals folks. Thank you all very much.'

In the evening Elvis Presley entertained 20,000 New Yorkers within the confines of the 'pig palace'. It was the first of four consecutive Madison Square Gardens concerts, each one enjoying standing-room-only audience figures. John Lennon, David Bowie, George Harrison, and Art Garfunkel were attracted to the Saturday evening session, which was recorded by RCA for album release – a mere eight days later. The move was undertaken to beat the bootleggers in their own field by getting the legitimate product on to the world market in record-breaking time.

Pleased that the 'New York Times' had described him as 'a champion – the only one in his class', Elvis left town and continued his tour on June 12th in Fort Wayne, and then Evansville, Milwaukee, Chicago, Fort Worth, Witchita, and Tulsa.

When Elvis returned to Memphis in July, the whole world was beginning to learn the truth concerning his marital split. No-one doubted that Presley would survive without Priscilla, but her departure seemed to encourage an uneasy atmosphere to settle upon the situation. But business as usual continued, and on August 4th Elvis' Summer Season commenced at the Las Vegas Hilton.

CHAPTER TEN

I'd like to acknowledge the presence of somebody in
the audience. There's a Fan Club that came all the
way from England here tonight. There's 200–250
of 'em here. I hope you enjoy the show, and thank
you for coming over!

Elvis' return each summer to Las Vegas was becoming a
safe-bet. His concerts were always set to conclude with the
start of America's Labor Day Holiday Jamboree (the first
Monday in September), and such 'security' was a blessing to
his overseas following. As Elvis Presley's return to live appearances some four or five years earlier hadn't precipitated
the expected 'world-tour', a consequential 'mountain to
Mohammed' situation had developed. Coachloads of fans from
all parts of the USA were not, as expected, filling the Hilton
showroom each night. Their demands were being catered for
almost on their own doorsteps with Elvis Presley's now
frequent nationwide tours. Overseas fans, however, couldn't
attend a concert in Fort Worth or Evansville because, chances
were, tickets would only go on sale for an hour or two, a couple
of weeks before the actual concert. Even out-of-State folks
would arrive in town too late for the last tickets. Las Vegas,
however, gave people months to plan ahead. The regularity of
Las Vegas gave Elvis' foreign following a chance to see their
idol.

No longer was the Showroom Internationale restricted to
grey-haired old men and their daughters, or the élite moneyed
middle-class America. Japanese, each with a forbidden camera,
sat alongside Scotsmen in kilts. Belgians out-tipped Australians
for the better seats. And the British – they began to add their
own distinctive touch to the place with comments along the
lines of, 'Is there anywhere in this town where you can get a
decent pint?' On the first visit to Las Vegas I once saw a wait-

ress ask a colleague to help with a translation of 'Eh, excuse me, duck. Can you tell us where the loo is?'

Rumours of a Las Vegas engagement gave us all time to plan, but we needed every valuable day in the preceding months if we were to be sure of being able to embark on our greatest adventure of all time. You see, we had decided to take 200 members of Elvis' British Fan Club to the States on Sunday, August 28th, 1972. It's not merely chartering an aircraft. You have to collect the money, arrange insurance, obtain visas, passports, licences, government approvals, government licences, pay taxes, collect taxes, arrange coaches, book meal stops, confirm room reservations, change hotel requirements, re-route coaches, obtain police approval, and then do it all over again, and more, for each passenger ... assuming of course you've been able to get an aeroplane. We had, and we were off at four o'clock in the morning.

Our World Airways 707 took 200 Elvis fans to the States for a fourteen-day trip into wonderland, and an in-flight champagne breakfast started off the fortnight of festivities. To satisfy certain international regulations governing air travel, and air-tour holidays we had to make three stops within the States, so we chose the South, Nevada, and California. Our first taste of American hospitality was manifested in the form of the US Immigration Officer, treating each British passport to the same respect enjoyed by a Proctor and Gamble 4p off soap coupon. Perhaps they had been warned by some friendly colleague at the London visa section of the US Embassy. Can you imagine all those visa application forms? Purpose of visit? 'To see the King.' State visible distinguishing marks: 'Elvis tattooed on my left buttock.' Residence while in the US – 'Heartbreak Hotel.'

In fact our first pension was a very pleasant up-market motel in Nashville. Fans were taken to see the Country Music Hall of Fame, The Grand Old Opry, and a recording of Porter Wagoner's WSM TV Spectacular with special guest-busty Dolly Parton. On our second day we headed for Elvisville, USA, and the opulance of hotel number two, the Memphis Peabody. A southern-style palace complete with reception lounge fountain, the daytime home for some half dozen live mallards. At 3.00 pm each day these ducks would leave their pond, walk along a red carpet, and board an elevator for a swift journey to that great duck pond in the sky – in fact, their 'penthouse' font on the roof of the twenty-storey hotel block. 'Graceland' was explored during the day, and the night-life in the evening offered more than its fair share of surprises. 'I've just been out with one of Elvis' cousins!' boasted one girl escorted back to the hotel by a more than usually friendly US cop. He replied, 'Honey, Elvis Presley has some two thousand cousins in this town for suckers just like you!'

On day four our air-conditioned coaches sped across the Tennessee border into Mississippi State and the small township of Tupelo and the Elvis Presley Birthplace. Our black driver joked nervously as we approached town, 'I don't rightly knows what I'm doin' here. They kick us blacks in the ass, as soon as look at us. Hey, you see that big red machine in the field right there. That machine will do in one hour what it took fifty niggers a whole day to do. It's a cotton picker. Ain't you glad they invented the machine? Well, here's your police escort. Here come de fuzz, here come de fuzz. Stick your finger out the window, and shout "right up de fuzz".' In fact we were about to enjoy a police escort from the chief of the Tupelo Police Dept., Ed Crider. Our people were then driven to the Elvis Presley Centre and a civic reception hosted by Mayor Ballard and Mrs Billy Boyd, boss of the gardens committee responsible for the Presley centre and restored homestead. Free police cycle pillion rides, shopping centre visits, and a walk across an actual cotton field preceded our return back to Memphis, and our driver's farewell recitation to the police escort. 'Bye bye de fuzz, bye bye de fuzz. Stick your finger, out the window, shout – "Right up de fuzz!"'

Wednesday, August 31st was a special day. Memphis was left behind as our United Airways jet headed towards Nevada, and if our British working-class background eyes had been widened in Tennessee, Las Vegas was to see all two hundred sets pop out. Everyone should visit Las Vegas, giving all a real reason to repent their sins. Las Vegas gives you a sneak preview of hell. Built on desert wastes, the town thrives on waste. Human beings waste their lives there. Visitors waste their time there. America wastes its energy there. Not to mention the millions of dollars an hour which are thrown away alongside convenience packaging in this, the world's greatest throwaway society. The great neon oasis lay before us, and our first chance to see Elvis Presley was looming nearer, and nearer.

When we touched down at the newly constructed airterminal, the inability of having to walk anywhere became apparent. Moving footways conveyed us to our destinations. Similar contraptions carried our belongings. Money machines beckoned our attentions. Win Win Win – Lucky Lucky Lucky – 21 21 21. We were still in the airport, and each bandit's single arm grasped at every passerby. 'Feed Me, Feed ME, FEED ME ! ! ! ! You might be luckyyyyyyyy.'

As soon as we left the environment-controlled, airconditioned security of the airport we all experienced desert heat for the first time. It was oh so hot, oh so warming, yet quite dry and really pleasant for a minute or two. Then the temperature excesses made one quickly tired, and somewhat depressed. Such daytime trauma could be overcome by staying in the hotel pool. While we ventured into the pool, Colonel Parker and Mr Diskin had made the three-mile journey from the Hilton to the Airport to greet us. We were early, they were late, and we missed each other, not knowing each's intentions.

The next day I was greeted with an early morning call. 'Todd, Todd, it's the Colonel. We missed you last night. Come to the hotel as soon as you can.' As the fans from Britain explored fantasyland, club staff and exalted guests (on our first trip we had met Tony Prince from Radio Luxembourg) met with the Presley management. Plans were made, plots were contrived, and everyone seemed socially acceptable to each other. 'Ian Bailye (Fan Club Staff), Tony Prince, and Todd Slaughter. You are all members of the *Snowman's League*. Respect your membership.' We were each given a card, a rule book, and a certificate by the Colonel, and our names were recorded. 'The Snowman's League', the club established by the Colonel, for little purpose other than to find work for an obscure printing company; had been known for years. Only membership of said society revealed its true intentions, and alas these are now confined within the secrecy of my masonic chest along with my Communist Party Membership Card and my Gay Lib badge. Well, these days, you have to cover all options, as well as keeping your hand over your ha'penny.

In the evening those with tickets took their first glimpse at Elvis Presley. Reservations were confined, four-hour-long queues were joined, and now we all prayed that no one would be disappointed. Come on Elvis, do your stuff. Please show us that our past nine months' work really wasn't in vain. There was no need to worry, of course he was a success. And there were 201 English people in the audience that night. 'A very good friend of mine, who has been trying to get me down pat for years, and hasn't made it yet – Tom Jones! I'm sorry Tom, you've either got it, or you don't. He knows I'm only kidding. He's one of the greatest entertainers in the world and a very good friend of mine.' We were all well pleased.

Las Vegas might have the advantage of being a safe venue for foreign fans to pin their hopes on, but its certainly an expensive exercise. The showroom ticket price of, say, £20 is just a fraction of what is finally handed over should a good seat be required. Tipping for Elvis concerts has reached heights of $1,000, so on this, our first USA trip, it was a nice surprise to enjoy prime seating for our last concert at normal prices, 'snowed' out of management by the Colonel. In addition to this first kindness, his unexpected $1,000 handout made our passengers' remaining days in the United States extra enjoyable. We put the gift towards a farewell USA party.

Following an on-stage introduction to our group by Tony Prince the disc jockey, a dozen or so hand-picked members of our party were lead back-stage to a Presley vestibule. As disciples, we waited nervously for our messiah, but when Elvis walked into the room his arrival was almost unnoticed. You see, he wasn't 12 feet tall, and he didn't have an aurora around his head, and as he entered his arrival wasn't greeted by a fanfare from the hidden 20th Century Fox orchestra. There were no searchlights scanning the sky either. 'I want to thank you folks for coming over. It's a wonderful job you're doing, and I just want to thank you. I'm sorry I won't be able to spend much time with you, as I've got a show to do, but I'll make sure it's a good one for your party. I've been trying to come over there for years now, but I guess I never made it. Someday I promise to come and see you all.' Although Elvis was still to dress for the show he did take time to answer a series of questions which were recorded, played back to those members of our party who asked them, and subsequently broadcast on Radio Luxembourg. 'I understand you want to know about my jumpsuits. Well, I dream up the designs, and then they go to work on 'em. They are designed for me by a guy called Bill Belew. Right now we're working on a new blues album in Memphis. We're getting the songs together, and a new film is due out soon, a follow up to "That's the Way It Is". That's about all we have planned for the moment. I still get a thrill out there. It's always like the first time. Every show is important to me, so I always try to make it like it's the first time.' Elvis was careful not to mention the contents of a press conference he was to host on the hotel's 30th floor after his closing show just six hours later.

Elvis had signed a contract for a world-wide television show. The first to be carried by live satellite linked up to a global audience, an idea which had been conceived by the writer ten years earlier when Telstar was launched and became the world's first orbiting communications satellite. In the early days of the 'Elvis Via Telstar' campaign a British television contractor had shown interest in the scheme, and even an American programmer wrote to the innovator in praise of the suggestion. However, when Jimmy Savile (British DJ) confronted Colonel Parker with a pilot suggestion the manager replied 'Why, the price I would charge would blast Telstar out of orbit.' The Colonel had obviously changed his mind, and Elvis spoke of the challenge of entertaining audience sizes beyond appreciation. 'It's very hard to comprehend after fifteen years; it's hard to comprehend that happening to all the countries all over the world. It's hard to comprehend. A live concert to me is exciting because of all the "electricity" which is generated in the crowd and on stage, but a live concert via satellite . . . I just hope I don't let them down in the satellite show. I'll have to exercise every day, vocalise every day. I do anyway, even if I'm working or not. So I'll just try to stay in shape.' Elvis concluded his address by answering one question concerning his marriage split. 'I have no plans to re-marry, but I have nothing against marriage. The break-up came about because of the pressure of my concert tours. It was just one of those things. It didn't work out, but we're still the best of friends.'

Apart from the British 'ambassadors', lots of guests packed the Hilton showroom that season, including Sammy Davis Junior, Paul Anka, and Richard Harris. Both Lisa and Priscilla were frequent visitors. Romance was in the air for Tom Diskin. He had earlier married an attractive lady called Yanique, and the couple honeymooned in the hotel. 'Miss Tennessee', a lady known otherwise as Linda Thompson, was beginning to make regular visits to Elvis' private hotel suite. But it was time for us to burst the showbiz bubble, and proceed further in a westerly direction. So on day 9 we arrived in Los Angeles. Well, we had seen the Southern States, flown across the Grand Canyon, visited the Hoover Dam, and seen Elvis. How could we leave the States without first seeing Disneyland? So our few remaining fun-filled days saw our passengers meeting Mickey Mouse, storming the 'Queen Mary' at a rested anchorage in Long Beach, eating lobster in Malibu, and partying on the last night in our Hollywood Hotel base, courtesy of Elvis and the Colonel. It seemed everywhere we went we were known as 'The Elvis Crowd', possibly because we could never go anywhere without Colonel Parker's third gift – an eight-feet-tall hound-dog. And it was this latter object plus fifty or so smaller 'brothers and sisters' bought by our passengers which caused a sizeable stir at Gatwick Airport, England, upon our return. On reflection, I'll never know why we bothered visiting Disneyland . . . we were Disneyland!

FOOTNOTE: This first Elvis Presley Fan Club charter to the States, organised by the British Fan Club, is now an annual operation. To date, almost two-thousand fan club members have made the journey to the USA to be entertained by their star.

CHAPTER ELEVEN

ALOHA FROM HAWAII

'I've never got over what they call stage fright. I go through it every show.'

As far back as April 1972 news had reached the press of Elvis Presley's intentions to appear before a world-wide audience on a satellite link-up. But the press reception at the end of his Hilton Summer Season now gave a definite date for the project – January 14th, 1973. RCA President Rocco Laginestra had already been in Europe a couple of months earlier to set up European transmissions, and now it was announced that USA audiences would see the concert live in a string of nationwide theatres using the Globcom commercial satellite system. Although the projected audience had reached frightening proportions, such a task didn't appear to worry Elvis, who preferred on this occasion to stay over in Vegas after his season at the Hilton. He spent his three-week vacation in the gambling town visiting other stars' shows – concerts he usually had to miss because of his own twice-nightly Hilton engagements.

By late September Elvis was in Beverly Hills. He had travelled to Los Angeles to put the final touches to a new movie, now retitled 'Elvis on Tour'. He went to the MGM studios to record general chit-chat segments which were to be dubbed and mixed into the movie's documentary dialogue. 'I always think about my performances, and I never completely feel comfortable with it. I don't let the people with me get comfortable with it either – I remind them that each audience is made up of a new crowd and they haven't seen us before, so it's gotta be like the first time we go on. I don't like to stay backstage too long. I've got to please the crowd, to excite them, to make them happy – I give myself to doing that show. If somebody walked up to me on stage and said "Hey, your head's just exploded" – I wouldn't hear them. A funny thing happened to me about a year ago. It was during an intermission, before my spot, and the lights were still on. I looked out and saw the crowd of people, and I just went weak at the knees. All of a sudden it scared me to death, 'cos I'm only used to going out when the house lights are all down. Right now, on tour we are doing two shows a night for five weeks. [After the shows] all the time we'll go upstairs and sing till daytime – gospel songs. I've done this from the time I was – I can't remember – two years old. It more or less puts your mind at ease – it does mine. In Las Vegas this is my way of "coming down". We sit around, and play to unwind. Since I was two all I've known was the Gospel music we all sang in Church with my family. That was music to me, it became part of my life. It was as natural as dancing, a way to escape from problems and my way of release. I can't say that I've been influenced by any other particular thing. I've been associated with rock 'n' roll, but I own records of Mario Lanza, and the Metropolitan Opera. I wouldn't have changed my career, except to say that my Hollywood image was wrong, and I knew it. I just couldn't do anything about it. I would get physically ill having to do all those movies. I'm not allowing any of my karate routines to be included in this movie. I don't want people to see the expressions on my face. I'm afraid that they might get the wrong impression of me.'

After the MGM session, Elvis returned to Graceland, only to fly back to Los Angeles a week or so later to attend a karate demonstration before embarking on his November tour. 'Burning Love' was now high in the world's hit parades, though Elvis himself confessed that musically it was a difficult number to reproduce in his stage act. However, he managed it on most dates, commencing on November 8th in Lubbock, Texas, and subsequently at dates at Tuscan, El Paso, Oakland, San Bernadino, and finally Long Beach, California. Daughter Lisa was accompanied by new-love Linda Thompson on the latter date. During this tour Elvis often competed against himself, playing at the same time as the release of MGM's 'On Tour'. Elvis had now reached Hawaii, and on November 17th he gave one show at the Honolulu International Centre, followed by two more the next day. On the 20th Elvis and the Colonel attended a press conference in the Rainbow Room of the Hawaiian Village Hotel when it was announced that ticket sales receipts at the time of the telerecording would be donated to the Kui Lee Cancer Fund. Kuiokalani Lee, who died in 1966, was the writer of the ballad 'I'll Remember You', and his widow, who stood by Elvis' side during the reception, sobbed when aware of their generosity. Colonel Parker also added $1,000 to the fund which finally reached some $75,000. ' "I'll Remember You" is a beautiful song. Everybody likes it – I do it everywhere. Although this is an international show, I guess I'll stick to English, although I've sung previously in Spanish and German. It's just a great privilege to do the satellite programme. I'm going to do my best – it'll be entertainment, there'll be no messages – I don't think that that's my job. I'll just try to make the people happy. As far as personal appearances in these places, I don't have any definite time, but I would like to come over to Europe, and to Japan.'

After the brief visit to Hawaii, Elvis flew back to Memphis, next to Las Vegas, and then returned home for Christmas to ready himself for the satellite spectacular.

'Aloha from Hawaii' was planned for transmission at 12.30 am on Sunday, January 14th, 1973, and this late hour (Hawaiian time) was selected so that the show would reach Japan's early evening high target audience. Though it was never admitted, the programme itself was made for the Far Eastern audiences and in particular to attract the huge revenue derived from the affluent Japanese sponsors. So millions upon millions of Eastern Hemisphere television viewers were now seen to be receiving preferential treatment from Elvis and the Colonel. Only a couple of European networks screened an edited relay version the following day, and the programme was never seen on British television. Such a shame as the concept was British.

The actual show opened with a telecine introduction of a morse-bleeped message animated to appear to come from the satellite. The picture then mixed to show a helicopter arriving at the Hawaiian village and out stepped Elvis wearing a white suit. He was met by Polynesian girls who greeted him with leis, while in the background the cultural centre's dancers

96

danced in the way every good Hawaiian girl should dance, though on this occasion to big band versions of 'Hound Dog' and 'All Shook Up'. The telecine picture was then mixed to a live transmission from Honolulu's International Centre Arena. Elvis' prologue theme 'Also Sprach Zarathustra' (Richard Strauss' introduction from the movie '2001 a Space Odyssey') was pumped out by the orchestra, and then on walked 'The King' wearing a white jumpsuit, embossed in red, blue, and golden stones arranged in dazzling eagle designs. He began his act with 'CC Rider' and continued by mixing old standards with his own hits, and brand new numbers, new even as part of Elvis' own repertoire. Conscious of the fact that the majority of his viewing audience that night understood little, if any, English, he kept his introductions to a minimum, though he did acknowledge the presence in the audience of Jack Lord, from TV's 'Hawaii Five-O' programme. This, however, was cut from the transmission, as Lord's programme appeared on a different network. Presley also thanked the producer: 'I'd like to thank our director and producer, Mr Marty Pasetta, for putting this show together. He's really done a fantastic job, him and his staff, and there's been a lot of people working on the show, and as you know – we're going out live. We're doing it on behalf of the Kui Lee Cancer Drive. We're supposed to raise $25,000, and tonight we have made that $75,000. So thank you!'

'Aloha from Hawaii' was beamed for almost one hour via the world's satellite networks, and a ninety-minute version of the show, taped at the same time as the transmission, was broadcast on the US networks later in April. The show was never simultaneously broadcast to US theatres, as originally announced. The split-screen technique used throughout the concert was much criticised, losing the impact it creates on big cinema screens. A double-album package, released by RCA, of the show's soundtrack attained the status of being the first (and possibly the only) quadrophonic album to sell one million copies.

Fresh from his Hawaiian success Elvis Presley opened a month long season on January 26th, again at the Las Vegas Hilton. It wasn't a series which went by without incident. On one occasion Elvis went hoarse during a concert and had to disappear off stage for twenty minutes, leaving Charlie Hodge, his 'fall guy', to fill in. He also had to cancel six of his midnight shows because of the 'flu. This was the season, too, when four men jumped up on stage during Presley's 'Suspicious Minds' routine and attempted to reach the singer. When they were 'restrained' by Red West and a couple of Hilton security staff they returned peacefully to their tables, only to file a suit against Elvis and the hotel for $4 million the following day. The four men from Peru claimed that they climbed on the stage only in an attempt to shake Elvis by the hand, and were subsequently beaten up by the star and his staff. 'In Las Vegas all singers have throat problems – it's called Desert Throat, and caused by the fact that there's no humidity in the air. Your vocal chords get very dry, and so you have to drink a lot of water. Recently, when we were over in Hawaii, we did a benefit for a cancer drive, and I met a gentleman I admire very much. He took us to his home, and I found him to be one of the nicest men I've ever met. Also, he's one of the greatest actors that ever lived – you know him from "Hawaii Five-O" ... Mr Jack Lord. Also I'd like to introduce you to one of my bodyguards – Red West. He was on the "Wild Wild West" TV series for two years. He was a stunt man, and he's been by my side for almost twenty years. We went to school together and he's one of my closest friends.'

On April 22nd Elvis embarked on yet another tour which was to take him back to Phoenix and then to Anaheim, Fresno, San Diego, Portland, Spokane, Seattle, finishing in Denver on April 30th. Four days later Elvis opened again at the Sahara Tahoe, in Lake Tahoe, an engagement which prevented him from taking part in a karate championship in San Francisco three weeks earlier. Elvis had wanted to be a competitor, but had to satisfy himself in the role of a spectator – his Tahoe contract prohibiting the star from taking part in any appearance within three hundred miles of the hotel. A chest infection caused Elvis to cancel his last three concerts. He flew back to Memphis, and recovered while relaxing and enjoying a few well-chosen midnight movie favourites.

June 20th saw him open a southern and eastern cities' tour in Mobile, with follow-up venues in Atlanta, Uniondale,

Pittsburg, Cincinatti, St Louis, back to Atlanta, then on to Nashville, Oklahoma City, and yet again back to Atlanta. Such had been the demand for tickets that a third Atlanta show was hurriedly tacked on to the end of the tour. During the tour, while in Mobile, Elvis telephoned Governor George Wallace (victim of an assassination attempt which subsequently confined the statesman to a wheelchair) to wish him well.

In July Elvis received his 7th degree black belt, and celebrated by going back into the studio – this time Elvis recorded at Stax in Memphis.

Elvis' year continued with the customary summer season commencing in Las Vegas on August 6th. Pet Clark and Lisa Minelli attended the opening show which was to start one of Elvis' most successful Las Vegas engagements. 'We love to sing. All of us up here love to sing and play music, and if it makes you happy ... They don't like us to stay on too long. The hotel don't like us on stage for more than fifty-five minutes, but we don't care what they like. Go and wake up Conrad (Hilton) and say "Get up. We got a show to do." Glenn Hardin (Elvis' piano player, and former member of the Crickets) quit last night ... 'cos I threw water on him. He came out with all the "arrangements" and all of his wardrobe and quit – made a big deal out of it. I'm gonna do it again tonight. Charlie Hodge does fantastic harmonies with me. He's been doing it for thirteen years now, and he does it so well that it's almost like one voice. In Las Vegas, things go backwards. You have breakfast in the evenings, and after you've been here a month, you don't know where ... when ... what ... who ... or ... why! We're not working for the money. We've got plenty of that. We're working to have fun, and if we can't get along ... then we might as well call it a day.' Elvis' latter comment was directed at one specific member of Elvis' staff. Elvis' British fan club were now making their second visit to the city, and in usual politeness Elvis greeted the visitors: 'For quite a few days there's been an English Fan Club here – 260 people from England – so I'd just like to say "hello". Just tell all those fans in England that I really love their devotion, and that we gotta come and see 'em. We got to. I've been saying it for years, but we will!'

Elvis remained in Vegas for a couple of weeks following the close of his season, and four weeks later he picked up his divorce papers. Three days later, on October 12th, Elvis arrived back in Memphis, but by 15th, as if reacting to the pressures of his marriage split, he was rushed into the Memphis Baptist Hospital with pneumonia, and was hospitalised until November 2nd. Afterwards Elvis convalesced in Los Angeles before returning to Memphis in mid-December for another Stax recording session. Lisa had come home to spend Christmas with her daddy, and she was escorted to the sessions by Linda Thompson.

1974, whilst very active for Elvis, brought forth few surprises and little change to the Presley calendar. Elvis returned to Las Vegas on January 26th and on March 1st commenced his longest ever tour starting off in Tulsa, and then visiting Houston for the Astrodome's annual Rodeo and Livestock shows. Here again Elvis played to sell-out audiences, although this time even these had increased to almost 45,000 for each of three concerts!!! The tour then moved to Monroe on March 4th, and then to Auburn, Montgomery, back to Monroe, then on to Charlotte, Roanoke, Hampton Roads, Richmond, Greesboro, Murfreesboro, Knoxville, Memphis, Richmond again, and Murfreesboro, with a final triumphant return concert in Memphis on March 20th, the latter being recorded for yet another live RCA album. Elvis had finally agreed to appear live in his own home town for the first time in thirteen years. He received a rapturous reception for each of his five Memphis concerts staged at the Mid South Coliseum. 'Hello Memphis! It's a pleasure to be home here for the first time in a long time. I'd like to tell you something if I could. It's always been said that a person cannot return (to entertain) in their own home town. But you have disproved that theory completely, and you have made it all worthwhile!' Alabama's Governor Wallace finally met Elvis Presley and made him an Honorary Colonel of his state. The Presley family had been criticised a few years earlier for giving support to the Wallace electoral campaign. The Governor was known to have strong right-wing views, and often thought to be racist. Elvis was horrified when he saw that 'Support Wallace' placards had been erected in the Graceland grounds, and he ordered their immediate removal. At the time he was quoted as saying, 'I'm just a singer. It is not my place to say anything about politics in any way which might influence the way my supporters might vote.'

More tours followed. Firstly a short Californian spree visiting San Bernadino on May 10th, Los Angeles on the 11th, Fresno on the 12th and back to San Bernadino again on the 13th. Dates 16 – 26th were reserved for a return to the Sahara Tahoe Hotel, and after a two-week break the singer was off again. This time Elvis played Fort Worth on June 14th and 15th before moving to Baton Rouge, Amarillo, Des Moines, Cleveland, Providence, Philadelphia, Niagara, Columbus, Louisville, Bloomington, Milwaukee, Kansas City, Missouri, Omaha, closing the tour in Salt Lake City on July 1st. Three days later Elvis was seen back in Memphis giving a karate display. Such stamina must have certainly added extra credibility to the benefits of the sport. Later that month Elvis made a private visit to Hawaii, then returned to Memphis by mid-August before going again to Las Vegas. Telly Savalas attended the opening show on August 19th, and proving that he could sell any record of Elvis, Colonel Parker had pressed a Presley talking album – issuing it on his own Boxcar label. Of course it sold, in sufficient quantities too to persuade RCA to re-press it themselves and add it to their own catalogue. It was a dreadful mix of pre-song introductions, produced without taste or conviction, an embarrassment even to Elvis' most loyal supporters. Halfway through the session Elvis caught the 'flu and missed two shows. 'I had a cold one day this week, and I had to quit. Had to miss two shows. This one night I had a temperature of 102°, and they wouldn't let me go on, 'cos with a temperature you lose your equilibrium and your balance and so forth. But in my entire nineteen years I've only missed six or seven shows. I love it out here. I know that people from all over come to see our shows. They fly, they drive, and there's not anyone on this stage, I MEAN ANYONE, that wouldn't rather be here than anywhere else in the world. To me a germ is an enemy! I hate the sonofabitch! I'll fight it. I went to hospital once because I had a little bronchial trouble in the tubes. You know what they do to you in hospital? They check you for everything in the world. They'll find something wrong with you. If they can't, they'll create something. They took a "liver balance". Do you know what a liver test is? Do you know what they do? The doctor comes in, asks you to turn your head, and takes a needle six inches long, and aaaaah – right between your ribs, and pulls out a piece of your liver. After this he says "Don't move for 24 hours!" And there I was – I was OK – I was getting well, and in he came and stabbed me. He looked like a Samurai warrior.'

Las Vegas – summer season '74 was certainly the season for Elvis to communicate to his audience. His act revolved around lengthy karate demonstrations, topped off with loads of home-spun philosophy. 'The other night there was a Minister in town to raise money for a new Evangelical Church. He had an all-night telethon (a marathon television fund raising programme) and J.D. Sumner and the Stamps went over and sang. The minister asked J.D. if maybe I would come by, and J.D. replied "If he does, I'll jump in the pool." Later I called and told the minister that because of my contract I can't appear in Las Vegas outside of the Hilton. But I told him I'd donate $2,500 if J.D. and the Stamps did jump into the pool. And they did. I told the minister I'd give another $1,000 if he'd jump in the pool. They had to throw him in! When I was a child I always wanted to be in a Gospel Quartet. When I was sixteen I went to the Ellis Auditorium in Memphis to an all-night Gospel session. I went alone because none of the other kids my age liked that kind of music. J.D. Sumner was then a member of the Blackwood Brothers Quartet. I never dreamed that someday I'd be on the same stage with him. I've known this man all the time since I was sixteen years old. He's been singing on stage for thirty-one years. He's the lowest bass singer in the world – goes down four keys off the piano keyboard. Now, I found these guys [pointing to the right] working in an upholstery shop in Nashville, Tennessee. I knew some of them years back. They'd formed a group and were working in the daytime and singing at night. I think they're fantastic! I brought them to Las Vegas with the act, and I call them 'Voice'.

'I couldn't have a better audience if I stood outside and

paid everyone $20 each to come in and listen. You're outa-sight! You see him – that's Charlton Heston, ladies and gentlemen. He's made some dilly, hasn't he? "Ben Hur", "The Ten Commandments" – I'll never forget that in my life. When he comes off that mountain, from Mount Sinai with those white tablets, and all that white hair. I'd like to talk to him sometime to find out what state of mind he had to get himself into to play that part. Can you imagine that? He had just talked to God, and came down the mountainside with those tablets under his arms and that white hair. I'd like to ask him how he got to thinkin' that part. Phew – it's tougher than a nickle stove-pipe. See that ring? I wore this ring on the "Aloha" special. It's not just one big diamond at all. The centre stone is $11\frac{1}{2}$ carats, and there are several diamonds surrounding it. It was a Christmas present to myself. I was looking for gifts for my father, my grandmother, and my daughter, and when the jeweller came – this just accidentally fell from his case. I was really suckered into buying it. It's the biggest diamond I've ever seen – I just thought I deserved it.'

'You know I've never liked the way this showroom's looked – the interior decorating. It's too wide for a performer. I had this ramp made so I could come out a little closer to the audience. Put a spotlight on to the statues on that wall. OK. That's nice. I don't know what it is, but that's nice. Tom Jones was in here the other night, and he's from Wales. I asked Tom who it was, and he said it was King Edward. King George, sorry, excuse me your majesty. Now take the spot-light and put it on those angels. Just look at those dudes, boy! Big fat angels. Put the spotlight on to this wall over here. You will notice a slight difference. Those of the Caucasian race. That's what it is, isn't it? Caucasian? It was on my Army draft card. I thought it meant "circumcised"! Anyway, the other night, I came down here at about 4.30 in the morning with a couple of friends who work for me – Jerry Schilling and Red West. Red is a 2nd degree black belt in karate – he's got a school in Memphis, and I'm very proud of him. Red wrote "Seperate Ways" and "Why Can't Everyday Be Like Christmas", and "If You Talk in Your Sleep". Anyway, he climbed the fence where they keep the supplies, the paint and

103

so forth, he climbed the fence, as high as this curtain; he went down and got a little can of black paint. He put it in his belt, came back, climbed over, and we went over there and stacked up two tables. I got up with the paint and brush, and I was Michaelangelo, or the guy that painted the ceiling in the Vatican – the Sistine Chapel. I painted that statue – it took thirty minutes to do. The hotel haven't said a word. I just thought I'd share it with you.'

'I have been involved in the art of Karate for some time – most people don't know to what extent. It's become to me like a way of life. I started doing it some sixteen years ago as a hobby, not as self-defence. It started in 1959 when I was in the Army. I study and learn every day for two to three, even six hours. It's helped me in self-control, body discipline, mind discipline, in my stage work, diet, and breathing techniques. It involves yoga. It involves meditation. Kung Fu and Karate are two different things. Kung Fu is slower – like sand blowing in your face. Karate is quicker – Karate gets on with it. There's a lot to do. It's not just breaking boards. The word "Karate", "kara" means open, and "te" means hand – open hand. It's an art, not a sport. It has a much deeper meaning. It involved the Buddhist monks. They had no way of protecting themselves from robbers, so evolved a way to keep themselves from being killed or robbed. They studied different animals. They studied the tiger. The tiger fights on its back. All cats do – your house cat does. They roll into a ball, and fight on their backs and you can't get near them. My Karate name is "Tiger". The cobra snake will approach its victim and mesmerise it, hypnotise it. The eagle is the highest flyer of all birds. He sees his prey, and comes out of the sky and gets his food in his all-powerful talons, and breaks bones and crushes its victim. They devised this over hundreds of years for humans to do it, using their hands, feet, legs, and elbows. I've never had to use it in my life in any violent way. It's not for that reason. On the contrary, it gives you self-confidence. It makes you a better citizen in your daily life. I'm sworn to a pledge never to use that which I have learnt to harm, frighten, or to disable. If so I could be stripped of my belt, and turned over to the law – the authorities.

'I teach – we have a class upstairs in my suite. We do it every day at six o'clock for about an hour and a half. In Los Angeles I study under Ed Parker, who teaches "kempo". In Memphis I study under a fellow who came from Korea, Mr Kang Rhee. Mr Rhee teaches the "pasaru" system, which means all systems in one. You take the best ingredients from all the systems. There's no age limit in this. Half the classes around the country are children, women, and older folk. They realise that this doesn't require tremendous physical strength. One man came to my instructors' school in Los Angeles. He was a business man in Beverly Hills and about fifty-four years old. He watched the class and told my instructors that he thought he was too old to go for his black belt. But the guy's been coming along every day in his lunch hours for two to three years, and now he's a black belt. You go through seven degrees before you get to the black-belt category. You test for each one of these. In 1960 I tested for my first-degree black belt. I had to fight two guys both at once and then separately. This one guy had a smile on his face all the time. I couldn't get near him. Next morning I was so sore, I couldn't get a comb through my hair. In 1963 I got the 2nd degree black belt. They skipped the 3rd and made me a 4th which carries the title "Associate Professor of the Art". The 5th degree holds the title "Professor of the Art". I got that four years ago. The 6th is "Senior Professor", and 7th "Associate Master". My 8th I got a few days ago and I now hold the title "Master of the Art." 9th degree would be "Senior Master of the Art", and 10th degree would be "Grand Master" and there are only a few of those guys in the world. You never hear about 'em. They don't appear on no TV shows, or in no black-belt magazines because they are trained as a religious order, a devotion, a way of life. Now that I've reached 8th degree I can start my own Karate Association. We are due to start our own style of Karate under the heading of the "American Karate Institute". We intend it to become an Americanisation of the art, using numbers 1, 2, and 3, in place of a foreign language.' Much of this 'lecture series' was witnessed by members aboard the British Fan Club's third USA charter – an interesting insight into an even more interesting entertainer!

By the end of the season Linda Thompson appeared to have been ditched in favour of a new petite blonde girl called Sheila Ryan who was also with Priscilla and Lisa.

Elvis was back in Memphis in mid-September for a further Karate demonstration, and on September 27th in Maryland he commenced his last tour for 1974. Other dates visited were Detroit, South Bend, St Paul, Detroit again, Indianapolis, Dayton, Wichita, and Abilene on October 9th. Two days later Elvis was back on the Sahara Tahoe stage fulfilling those shows he had had to cancel through illness the previous year.

CHAPTER TWELVE

BACK IN THE 'OLD' ROUTINE

On January 8th, 1975 it was time for Elvis to crack open his first carton of Phyllosan – the 'King' had reached the magical age of 40! No longer could he maintain his 'Peter Pan' image, and in fact his form too was beginning to suffer a bit. Advancing years had never previously worried Elvis, though on this occasion he preferred to hide away from the camera crews who had arrived outside the Graceland driveway. In the evening Elvis held a small birthday dinner party for just the immediate family and his close friends. Linda Thompson was in attendance as his 'lady in waiting' and all present reported that it was a quiet 'do'.

Because the Hilton was trying to outgrow the recently constructed MGM Grand complex, Elvis' usual January season had been put off until springtime. By then the hotel moguls would have added an extra tower block, regaining its position of being the Biggest in Town! It was just as well, because Elvis was re-admitted to the Memphis Baptist Hospital at 4 o'clock in the morning of January 29th. He was suffering from a twisted colon, and was confined to the isolation of a hospital suite where even daylight was excluded by aluminium foil coated windows. During his stay in hospital his father, Vernon Presley, suffered a heart attack and was admitted to the same hospital. Elvis was allowed to leave at midnight on February 13th. Elvis' hospitalisation was now becoming a regular occurrence. All kinds of stories filled the newspapers, and his impending death was predicted now on a weekly basis. Possibly the story nearest to the truth centres around Elvis' water retention problems, and his visits to hospital were more to relieve the strains incurred by the malady than any miracle cure. Only constant rest and continual attention could prevent the illness, and Elvis hadn't the time to enjoy either. During convalescence he bought himself a yellow Panterra sports car, and played squash at a new raquet-ball health club. He also acquired five new horses. At the beginning of March he was busy working in RCA's Los Angeles studios, his last visit there to date.

Elvis opened at the Hilton in Las Vegas on March 18th, but not every member of the packed house attended in the hope of seeing a roly-poly-Presley! Instead they saw a roly-poly-Parker. The Colonel dressed up as Santa Claus and walked on stage carrying Elvis' young Chow 'Getio', as the band played 'Jingle Bells', Conrad Hilton attended the dinner show, which was to herald the opening of the hotel's new wing extension on April 1st.

After the season ended, Elvis went to Nashville for more recording and a week or so later he commenced yet another tour on April 24th in Macon. Then he moved to other southern cities such as Jacksonville, Tampa, Lakeland, Murfreesboro, Atlanta, Monroe, Lake Charles, Jackson and back to Murfreesboro, closing on May 7th. Proceeds from the Jackson concert on May 5th were donated to a fund set up to benefit the victims of a tornado which hit McComb, Mississippi the day after Elvis' 40th birthday. He raised over $100,000. Between tours Elvis received a Ju-Jitsu Federation award for 'Outstanding Achievement in the Art', and then embarked on tour number two in Southland on May 30th. He also executed concerts in Huntsville, Mobile, Tuscaloosa, Houston, Dallas, Shreveport, Jackson, and returned to Memphis' Mid South Coliseum for one show on June 10th.

On June 16th Elvis was back in hospital. This time he was undergoing treatments for possible glaucoma – an eye infection. Now we were to read that not only was Elvis eating himself to death, he was going blind too. In fact it was a miracle he stayed alive at all because so many newspaper men were trying to bury him. The third leg of Elvis' summer tour commenced on July 8th in Oklahoma City, Haute Terre, Cleveland, Charleston, Niagara Falls, Springfield, New Haven, Cleveland again, Uniondale, Norfolk ('I always say Nor-fork. Now that's wrong. The Norsemen came down here – it was named for them; North Folk. It's Nawfulk!'), Greensboro, and finishing on June 24th in Asheville, North Carolina. The management of the Rodeway Inn in Asheville, host to the Presley entourage, cut up the bed linen when the troupe left town and offered the bits in a charity sale.

Elvis was now giving away gifts to all and sundry. At the Asheville concerts one fellow in the audience was tossed Elvis' guitar, and another 'won' a six and a half thousand dollar diamond ring. D. J. Sumner was gifted with another Presley ring – this one worth more than $40,000, and a few days later, on Sunday night July 27th at 10 pm, a black lady was given a white and gold Cadillac Eldorado as she admired Elvis' own car parked on the Madison Cadillac lot at Union Avenue, Memphis. 'You can't have that – it's mine. But never mind, I'll buy you another. Go into the showroom and pick out the one you like.' She also received a cheque and clothing to go with the gift.

Elvis' 13th season in Las Vegas was certainly unlucky for Elvis. He started off the schedule on August 18th adopting a new format, and audience requests determined the numbers he would include in the act. It was a nice idea, and Elvis liked it too. 'There's more freedom doing the show. We didn't re-hearse. The audience seem to like it – I think one reason why is that they're picking the songs. Sometimes that causes a prob-lem for me because I can't remember the words to every song. What people don't realise is that they actually 'help' me when they react to my singing.' This additional audience contact helped with the humour on occasions. Once when he was kiss-ing a short-haired girl in the audience he remarked that her head reminded him of Kojak first thing in the morning, before he does his TV shows – with a little bit of hair. 'I remember when I was working at Paramount on a movie, Telly Savalas was there, and so was Yul Brynner. When I'd go into makeup in the morning I'd hear the sounds of electric razors first thing each morning. Both actors were shaving their heads!' On August 21st Las Vegas awoke to the news that through illness Elvis had cancelled his Hilton season. With indecent haste the hotel removed all the billboards and Presley paraphernalia from the Greater Las Vegas area, and a stand-in was found for the remaining season. Elvis fans who had travelled to Las Vegas from all parts of the globe were heartbroken. Included in that total were 250 members of the Official Elvis Presley Fan Club of Great Britain. After his illness Elvis decided to sell his Palm Springs home, leaving him with no permanent base on the West Coast. But he was able to acquire a couple of 'planes, and possibly even a third as a short-term investment. Plane number one was an 880 Corvair, a four-engined jet formerly owned by Delta Airways. The inside passenger accommodation was gutted and luxury trappings were replaced into the empty shell. Its livery included the 'TCB' motif, and she was named 'The Lisa Marie' operating under the call sign of 'Hound Dog One'. 'Hound Dog Two' was a twin-engined executive jet, also called 'Lisa Marie' and operated by the Presley fleet.

Elvis had now to fulfil his oustanding Las Vegas commitment, and a period, generally the slackest in Las Vegas' annual schedule, was selected—the first two weeks of December. The move was perfect. It suited Elvis, it suited Vegas, and surprisingly it suited Elvis' fans. Perhaps this new slot would become a permanent fixture for Elvis' annual appearances in Nevada State.

Elvis returned to Memphis on December 17th and stayed until Boxing Day when he departed Graceland for Pontiac, a town near Detroit in Michigan. Here, on New Year's Eve, Elvis put on a concert which grossed $800,000, over a half a million pounds – an all-time record – when he appeared before some 60,000 people all crammed inside the huge covered stadium. At midnight, Elvis joined in with the crowd to sing 'Auld Lang Syne' and a few minutes later brought the audience to its feet with a patriotic rendering of 'America The Beautiful'. It was now 1976 – the 200th birthday year of the United States. 'As you see, I've ripped my pants! 60,000 people, and they'll all see what I've got under my pants! I'd like to tell you it's a pleasure to be here, and if I appear nervous it's because I am. You know this is the largest audience we have ever played to – and I have to go and rip my pants . . .'

With the sale of his remaining Los Angeles property, Elvis had no alternative residence to Graceland in Memphis, so in January he went 'house hunting', and his quest took him to Colorado. Elvis and employees were staying at Vail – an exclusive skiing resort some 100 miles west of Denver – and the singer reported that he would like to live in the area. Newspapermen eventually tracked him down, but were disappointed that Elvis was never to be seen on the snow slopes. That was because the Presley clan were restricting their skiing to the dark hours ... a point not overlooked by one enterprising photographer who captured Elvis clad in ski suit and mask, looking more like the Abominable Snowman than the king of rock 'n' roll. During a visit to Denver Elvis' generosity brought citicisms from the City Fathers. His gifts of expensive Lincolns and Cadillacs to Denver police officers was thought to be injudicious.

Girl-friend Linda Thompson, who had accompanied the party to Vail, left the Presley camp before the end of the vacation to audition for TV work in Los Angeles. Although Elvis didn't spend his birthday at home, it didn't prevent the people of Memphis expressing their good wishes in their usual abnormal manner. Department stores displayed greetings messages on their marquees, and the public address system at Memphis Airport informed all passengers arriving in the city that January 8th, 1976 was Elvis' 41st birthday. The fact that Elvis steals much of the city's own limelight has always given rise to a love-hate relationship from the citizens of Memphis. Those that love Elvis worship the man. Those that hate him, ever conscious of his presence in the city, would sooner he moved to another town. Still, whether they liked having him there or not, Elvis returned to Memphis during the first week of February to record album tracks in his Graceland basement studio. Extensions to the Presley mansion had now included a squash court, and this addition was to pave the way for another business venture to be known as 'Presley Centre Courts Inc.' The company, based on Popular Avenue, was chaired by Elvis with his personal medic Dr Nichopoulos the president, and Joe Esposito vice-president. It was the intention of the board to open a string of raquetball courts throughout the Southern States, but Elvis sold off his interest after only six months.

Elvis' annual tour schedule meant that the star would appear before one and a half million people each year. 1976 was to be no exception and he opened his season on March 17th with three concerts in Johnson City, moving to Charlotte, Cincinatti, and finishing six days later on March 22nd in St Louis, a total of eight concerts. Tour number two opened in Kansas City on April 21st and then travelled to Omaha, Denver, San Diego, Long Beach, Seattle, and concluding in Spokane on April 27th – nine appearances. Three days later Elvis began a ten-day residence at the Sahara Tahoe in North Nevada. After a two-week break, tour number three visited Bloomington on May 27th, and then the Iowa town of Ames, Oklahoma City, Odessa, Lubbock, Tucson, El Paso, Fort Worth, finishing on June 4th, 5th and 6th in Atlanta Georgia, a further total of eleven dates.

Concert tour four opened on 25th June in Buffalo, then to Providence Largo, Philadelphia, Richmond, Greensboro, Shreveport, Baton Rouge, Fort Worth, Tulsa, and finishing back home at the Mid South Coliseum on July 5th, eleven more concerts.

Tour five, commencing on July 23rd, saw off fifteen concerts spread over ten new towns including Louisville, Charleston, Syracuse, Rochester, Syracuse again, Hartford, Springfield, New Haven, Hampton Roads, Roanke, and concluding in Feyetteville in Alabama.

Traditionally, late August would see Elvis in Las Vegas, but it was announced that his season at the Hilton would from now on occupy the pre-Christmas holiday period, just after 'Thanksgiving'. Even at attempt to play Elvis at the Las Vegas Convention centre was aborted, possibly due to Elvis' Hilton contract, leaving him little room to manoeuvre in the gambling city. So another series in Elvis' bi-centennial whistle-stop celebrations saw the 'King' in San Antonio on August 27th and then Houston, Mobile, Tuscaloosa, Macon, Jacksonville, Tampa, St Petersburg, Lakeland, Jackson, Huntsville, and in Pine Bluff, Arkansas on September 8th when tour six closed ... 15 appearances.

Elvis' October tour commenced on the 14th for three dates in Chicago, and then on to Duluth, Minneapolis, Sioux Falls, Madison, South Bend, Kalamazoo, Champaign, Cleveland, Evansville, Fort Wayne, and finally Dayton on October 26th. That was tour seven with 14 concerts. And finally just before Elvis' first and only Las Vegas season in 1976, November 24th and 25th in Reno, 26th Eugene, 27th Orallis, 28th San Francisco – five more towns.

All in all, during 1976 Elvis Presley was to appear on tour in almost 90 different locations, plus ten days at the Sahara Tahoe, and 15 concerts in the Las Vega Hilton. So if we say that an average concert audience is made up of some 15,000 people, and that the showroom audiences at Tahoe and Vegas average out at 2,000 per session, then during 1976 Elvis must have performed before a total audience of over ONE MILLION FIVE HUNDRED THOUSAND persons – grossing something in the region of $12,000,000. Some achievement for a man, who in the eyes of the press, is a 'has-been'.

Elvis concluded his year in Las Vegas. He opened his Hilton season on December 2nd and finished on the 12th, playing to a multi-national audience throughout the engagement. 'Ladies and Gentlemen. I'd like to bring something to your attention. Today there are 400 people from England who came in here specially to see the show. They gave me this award and it's a gold record – and I'd like to welcome them here. The gentleman that brought them over, his name is Todd Slaughter, and (from the London 'Daily Mirror') Clifford Davis. Thank you – and I hope you have a good time. (You want to know) when I am coming to England? Listen – it's being prepared now. It really is. We really are – we really are. It just takes a while to arrange. We're going to Canada too!'

And so it goes on. Elvis jokes with his following, performs to record-breaking sell-out audiences, and throws away any personal private life he might have left, giving his all to his public. 1977 sees another year of concert tours on an even more frequent basis than before. Now Elvis is on the road for two weeks, rests for ten days, and then he's off again on another 14-day stint. Girl-friend Linda Thompson, who for a time was de-throned by Sheila Ryan, is again swopped for a new beauty, Ginger Alden. Newspapers continue to use photographs which might well have been taken using anamorphic lenses, and their editors refusing to use any picture which might be construed as flattering. Still, it's some consolation if after twenty or so years the only criticism the press can throw up at your professional life is your apparent inability to be able to control your own weight.

113

CONCLUSIONS

I do not think I am in a position to criticise Elvis Presley, nor do I find it pertinent to attack his management. We all have our own ideas on how we might have reshaped Elvis' career, but faced with the actual dilemma I doubt that few amongst us have even a tenth of the talents of Colonel Parker.

Elvis was launched on to the American music scene at the time of the birth of the American Dream. Schools in California were having car parks added to their facilities, and the youth of the USA had money enough to experiment in this new music trend. The creation of 'Elvis Presley' the product happened at this precise moment. A year earlier the plot would have mis-fired. A year later Elvis may well have been beaten to the post.

Elvis Presley was the world's first popular music super-star. When Elvis was getting exposure on television in 1956 half of America wanted to have nothing to do with the guy, whilst the other half wanted to sleep with him. In those early days his appeal was nothing short of explosive, with the resultant shrapnel piercing hearts, minds and morals.

To keep the star away from the public, a private army of friends and companions was used, forming an impregnable line of defence. Inside the human barricade Elvis was 'free' to live what was left of his personal life in reasonable seclusion. As pop music has progressed in the past two decades, stars of almost similar magnitude have learnt that they don't have to live the life of the recluse to survive, and that socialising with Mr General Public isn't that prohibitive. Elvis, of course, having gone so far, cannot retrace such steps, and must continue in his Howard Hughes environment. It might appear to be an enormous human waste, but at the time, who would have dared to have chosen a different course?

Apart from the die-hard establishment, after Elvis Presley completed his national service, he held the entertainment world in the palm of his hand. Elvis and the Colonel chose to exploit the movie industry box office. Were they wrong? Would Elvis be as big today had both parties chosen television? Obviously we have no idea, though most believe Elvis would have benefitted from this additional media.

In his time, Elvis has recorded more than his fair share of rubbishy material, though it must be argued that so has every other artiste. In his favour the 'King' can add that his bad repertoire is confined to movie soundtracks – a period in his career over which he chose to exert no control. Perhaps Elvis should have refused such trite scripts and melodies, but when the royalty cheques are embossed with a string of zeros who but a fool would turn away from a crock of gold? Besides, when the only people you associate with keep telling you what a wonderful job you're doing – in anticipation of being able to hold on to their own treasured positions – after a few years you are bound to think that you are almost perfect.

Elvis' return to live entertainment was welcomed from almost all quarters, but outside of the United States, and away from the activity of fan club organisation, the public is under the illusion that Elvis Presley has possibly retired. Helplessly out-of-date musicals seen on television appear today to be nothing but corn, though when first released they were the personification of Elvis' greatness. Elvis might top the hit parades from time to time, but the importance of such a meter of success has diminished since the demise of the Beatles. Those in the business today try to 'con' the public into believing that our new sounds are part of an art form far removed from the early attempts of Elvis Presley and his contemporaries. How wrong they are, and they will be proved to be so, when in fifty years' time the name of Elvis Presley will still be known when acts like Bowie, E.L.O., Pink Floyd, and Status Quo have long been forgotten.

Perhaps as fans we have all been guilty of building Elvis Presley into a bigger star than he actually would have liked to have been. Let's face it, until recent years we have never allowed even the slightest brickbat the opportunity to come home to roost. Such adoration has created an image even a super-human-being would have difficulty in living up to, and we have given Elvis Presley such a burden.

I have the greatest respect for Colonel Parker, and the

highest admiration for Elvis Presley. I respect the Colonel for having the guts to steer Elvis through comparatively uncharted waters, and I admire Elvis for staying on course in spite of many rough seas and stormy weather.

If I could be granted one wish in respect to Elvis' career, I would like to see Presley, the man, physically spend more of his time taking an interest in his fan clubs. I don't want that statement to appear to intimate that fan club secretaries like myself should benefit from such preferential treatment, but with no press officer and no published contact address we are the only source of legitimate news for fans and the media alike. We are the only contact between Elvis and his followers, and apart from limited record company assistance, our efforts are self-generated. When an Elvis Presley news story breaks through an agency, I'm the person got out of bed at five o'clock in the morning by the BBC. I'm the person who has to eat his Sunday lunch whilst speaking on the telephone to UPITN, and I'm the person who is asked by RCA Great Britain if I know of any impending record releases.

Elvis has preferred to leave fan clubs alone, hoping that all will survive on their own integrity. Perhaps he feels that fan club secretaries would take advantage of such a liaison, and I have no doubt that that would happen. But in return doesn't Elvis have a network of unpaid press officers throughout the world?

In recent months a fan club president in the States bitterly complained of the absence of co-operation from within the Presley camp, and for the first time someone within the said camp dared to venture a reply. Elvis' personal secretary, Miss Pam Parker, explained to the affronted fan club boss that their club was given 'all the co-operation that was ours to give.' She went on to explain our love of Elvis Presley. 'Do you know how the Bible defines really loving and caring? Love is very patient and kind, never jealous or envious, never boastful or proud, never haughty or selfish or rude. Love does not demand its own way. It is not irritable or touchy. It does not hold grudges, and will hardly even notice when others do it wrong. It is never glad about injustice, but rejoices whenever truth wins out. If you love someone (like Elvis) you will be loyal to

116

him no matter what the cost. You will always believe in him, always expect the best of him, and always stand your ground in defending him. All the special gifts and powers from God will someday come to an end, but love goes on *forever* (I Cor. 13: 4–8 paraphrased).

'You speak of running into selfish attitudes, and so called "number one fans", and ego maniacs etc. Well, perhaps some are but I say, "And why beholdest thou the mote that is in thy brother's eye, but considerest not the beam that is in thine own eye? (Matt. 7:3).

'Blame us as employees if you must, and think we don't take enough responsibility or too much as "gestapo", whichever you choose to believe. But don't you dare malign a man (like Elvis) who has given of himself to so many, and is not to blame . . .'

And there you have it. Like myself, and Pam Parker, you may possibly agree that Elvis really has sold his soul for rock 'n' roll. Elvis has given his all in exchange for the love he'll never receive; money, he can never spend; and immortality he will never live to appreciate. Like Disney, Presley will bequeath this world his heritage.

Elvis Presley's mortal future will remain as big a mystery as his immortal past. It is known he finds his relief from the workday strains in privately performing the gospel music catalogue. Elvis might escape from his world and become a Gospel Singing Preacher. He might extend his karate prowess, reaching for his 9th degree belt, and perhaps even considering the solitude of 10th degree supremacy. But it is more likely that he'll continue to sing his way through the saga of his life, admitting to all that he has 'One Broken Heart for Sale.'

THE END

APPENDIX 1

ELVIS' RECORD SALES ACHIEVEMENTS

When Enrico Caruso sold one million copies of his record, the Victor Talking Machine Company awarded the singer with a solid gold replica of the original recording. Since then the music industry has acknowledged sales performances by issuing 'gold' and 'silver' records. Today these awards are manufactured from old matrix (pressing dies) and either plated or sprayed the desired colour.

In Britain a silver disc is awarded to singles selling 250,000 copies. A 'gold' record is issued to acts whose record sells half a million. More recently a 'platinum' disc has been given to mark the one millionth sale.

Long playing records receive different awards. A gold disc is sometimes given to an artiste for a mere 100,000 units. A silver album for £100,000's worth of sales. (In Norway an album will 'go gold' for just 20,000 sales, a single 50,000. In Holland a gold single will be earned by a sales achievement of 100,000 copies.)

An album in the States now receives the gold trophy after $1,000,000's worth of sales, though this may only mean that less than 200,000 copies have been sold.

Elvis Presley is thought to have sold 450 million records. Some companies allow 1 LP to represent 5 singles, though it is understand that RCA USA count an album only as 'one' record. Consequently when measured against other artistes – whilst Elvis is still ahead – the margin is artificially narrow.

For example, the TV promoted product 'Elvis 40 Greatest', released in the UK by Arcade records, sold 2,500,000 units! As this was a double album package, we could say 5 million actual albums. Multiply that figure by the industry's mythical 5 and Elvis could have sold 25 million singles when represented in terms of this album's mammoth sales. The total sales value of this item has topped $16 million – and that

achievement by any artiste on any label is unequalled anywhere in the world.

It has been said that Elvis Presley may have reached a total
retail sales value of some $850,000,000 and on a dollar-for-
dollar basis (a single in the States sells for $1) that would re-
present 850 million singles.

As far as RCA are concerned, though the figure is 450
million, and whilst one might expect that he owns some 400
gold discs, the figure is more likely to be less than a hundred.

APPENDIX 2

ELVIS' BRITISH FAN CLUB

The Official Elvis Presley Fan Club of Great Britain and the
Commonwealth is the world's largest Presley fan club. With a
membership figure in excess of 12,000 the club recently celebrated it's 21st Birthday.

Each new member receives a membership card, an intro-
ductory letter and a fan club magazine packed with news and
pictures about Elvis Presley, the fan club, its activities, special
offers, and members' services. Magazines are despatched to
members at regular two-monthly intervals. A comprehensive
branch leader network operates throughout the UK, and during the year local branch secretaries stage regular get-togethers,
parties, coach outings to fan club events and film specials.

The British Fan Club has an active travel service. In recent
years members have been taken to Belgium, Holland, France,
Germany and Luxembourg for winter-break mini holiday pro-
motions. The annual USA charter – a two week inclusive tour
of the United States including Presley in concert – usually
visits Nashville, Memphis, Tupelo, Las Vegas, Hollywood, Los
Angeles and San Francisco.

Nearer to home, the fan club organises film shows in major
UK centres, and in the summer each year there's the Elvis
Convention. Attracting over 2,000 fans, this special show is
organised in aid of the Guide Dogs for the Blind Association.
Guests who have supported the function include Jimmy Savile,

Tony Prince, Rosko, Kid Jensen, Anita Harris, Paul Burnett, Spencer Davis and Alvin Stardust. Radio Luxembourg, the BBC, ITV, French, German and Dutch TV, as well as MGM have frequently featured highlights of this annual event. The British fan club has raised over £6,000 for charity.

Readers requiring further details should send a stamped addressed envelope to Elvis Presley Fan Club, P.O. Box 4, Leicester.

APPENDIX 3

ELVIS PRESLEY'S RECORDING HISTORY

UK SINGLES. All released on RCA unless otherwise indicated.

1956	Heartbreak Hotel/I was the one	(HMV)
	Blue suede shoes/Tutti Frutti	(HMV)
	I want you, I need you, I Love you/	
	My Baby left me	(HMV)
	Hound dog/Don't be cruel	(HMV)
	Blue Moon/I don't care if the sun don't shine	(HMV)
	Love me tender/Anyway you want me	(HMV)
1957	Love me/Mystery train	(HMV)
	Mystery train/I forgot to remember to forget	(HMV)
	Baby let's play house/Rip it up	(HMV)
	Playin' for keeps/Too much	(HMV)
	All shook up/	
	That's when your heartaches begin	(HMV)
	Paralysed/When my blue moon turns to gold	(HMV)
	Lawdy Miss Clawdy/Tryin' to get to you	(HMV)
	Loving you/Teddy bear	
	Gotta Lotta Livin' to do/Party	
	Santa bring my baby back/	
	Santa Claus is back in town	
1958	I'm left, you're right, she's gone/	
	How do you think I feel	(HMV)
	Jailhouse rock/Treat me nice	(HMV)
	I beg of you/Don't	(HMV)
	Wear my ring around your neck/	
	Dontcha think it's time	(HMV)
	Hard headed woman/Don't ask me why	(HMV)

	King Creole/Dixieland Rock	(HMV)
	All shook up/Heartbreak hotel	(HMV)
	Hound dog/Blue suede shoes	(HMV)

1959 One Night/I got stung
     A fool such as I/I need your love tonight
     A Big hunk of love/My wish came true

1960 Stuck on you/Fame and fortune
     A Mess of blues/The girl of my best friend
     It's now or never/Make me know it

1961 I gotta know/Are you lonesome tonight
     Wooden heart/Tonight is so right for love
     Surrender/Lonely man
     Wild in the Country/ I feel so bad
     His latest flame/Little Sister

1962 Rock-a-Hula Baby/I can't help falling in love
     Good luck charm/Anything that's part of you
     She's not you/Just tell her Jim said Hello
     Return to sender/Where do you come from

1963 One broken heart for sale/
        They remind me too much of you.
     Devil in disguise/
        Please don't drag that string around
     Bossa Nova Baby/Witchcraft
     Kiss me Quick/Something Blue

1964 Viva Las Vegas/What'd I say
     Kissin' cousins/It hurts me
     Such a night/Never ending
     Ain't that loving you baby/Ask me
     Blue Christmas/White Christmas

1965 Do the Clam/You'll be gone
     Crying in the chapel/
        I believe in the man in the sky
     Tell me why/Puppet on a string
     Blue river/Do not disturb

1966 Please don't stop loving me/
        Frankie and Johnny
     Love letters/Come what May
     All that I am/Spin out
     If every day was like Xmas/
        How would you like to be

1967 Indescribably Blue/Fools fall in love
The love machine/You gotta stop
Long legged girl (With the short dress on)/
    That's someone you'll never forget
There's always me/Judy
Big Boss man/You don't know me

1968 Guitar man/High heel sneakers
US Male/Stay away
You'll never walk alone/We call on Him
A little less conversation/Almost in love

1969 If I can dream/Memories
In the Ghetto/Any day now
Clean up your own backyard/
    The fair's moving on
Suspicious minds/You'll think of me
Don't cry Daddy/Rubberneckin'

1970 Kentucky rain/My little friend
The wonder of you/Mama liked the roses
I've lost you/The next step is Love

1971 You don't have to say/Patch it up
There goes my everything/
    I really don't want to know
Rags to riches/Where did they go Lord
Heartbreak hotel/Hound Dog/
    Don't be cruel   (Maxi)
I'm leaving/Heart of Rome
Jailhouse rock/Are you lonesomeTonight/
    Teddy Bear/Steadfast, Loyal, True   (Maxi)
I Just can't help believing/
    How the Web was woven

1972 Until it's time for you to go/
    We can make the morning
American Trilogy/
    The first time ever I saw your face
Burning Love/It's a matter of time
Separate ways/Always on my mind

1973 Polk Salad Annie/See See Rider
Fool/Steamroller blues
Raised on rock/For ol' times sake

1974	My Boy/Loving arms
1975	Promised land/It's midnight
	Green green grass of home/
	Thinking about you
	T-r-o-u-b-l-e/Mr Songman
	Blue Moon/You're a heartbreaker/
	I'm left, you're right, she's gone (Maxi)
1976	Hurt/For the Heart
	Girl Of My Best Friend/Mess of Blues
	Suspicion/Long Lonely Highway
1977	Moody Blue/She Thinks I Still Care
	All Shook up/Heartbreak Hotel
	Jailhouse Rock/Treat Me Nice
	I Got Stung/One Night
	A Fool Such As I/I Need Your love Tonight
	It's Now Or Never/Make Me Know It
	Are You Lonesome Tonight/I gotta Know
	Wooden Heart/Tonight is so right for Love
	Surrender/Lonely Man
	His Latest Flame/Little Sister
	Rock a Hula Baby/Can't Help Falling In Love
	Good Luck Charm/
	Anything That's Part Of You
	She's Not You/
	Just Tell Her Jim Said Hello
	Return To Sender/
	Where Do You Come From
	Devil In Disguise/
	Please Don't Drag That String Around
	Crying in the Chapel/
	I believe In The Man In The Sky
	The Wonder of You/Mama Liked The Roses

FOOTNOTE: Whilst years ago it was record company policy to maintain a complete catalogue of single releases, modern marketing techniques remove singles from company lists after 18 months to 2 years.

As virtually all the hit parade tracks are subsequently contained on compilation albums the need for keeping every single in catalogue is no longer necessary.

UK ALBUMS. All released on RCA unless otherwise indicated.

1956	Rock 'N' Roll No. 1	(HMV)	DD
1957	Rock 'N' Roll No. 2	(HMV)	DD
	The Best of Elvis	(HMV)	DI
	Loving You		DI
	Elvis's Christmas Album		DI
1958	King Creole		
	Elvis Golden Records		
1959	Elvis		
	A Date with Elvis		II
1960	Elvis Gold Records (Vol. 2)		
	Elvis is back		
	GI Blues		
	His Hand in Mine.		
1961	Something for everybody		DI
	Blue Hawaii		
1962	Pot Luck with Elvis		II
1963	Rock 'N' Roll No. 2		
	Girls, Girls, Girls		II
	It happened at the World's Fair		II
	Fun in Acapulco		II
1964	Elvis's Golden Records (Vol. 3)		
	Kissin' cousins		II
	Roustabout		II
1965	Girl Happy		II
	Flaming star and Summer kisses		DD
	Elvis for Everyone		
1966	Harem Holiday		II
	Frankie and Johnny		II
	Paradise Hawaiian style		II
	California Holiday		II
	How Great Thou Art		
1967	Double Trouble		II
1968	Clambake		II
	Elvis Gold Records (Vol. 4)		
	Speedway		II
1969	Elvis Sings Flaming Star		DI
	Elvis (NBC TV SPECIAL)		DI
	From Elvis in Memphis		

124

1970	Let's be friends	DI
—	From Memphis to Vegas/	
—	From Vegas to Memphis	
—	On Stage	
	Elvis Christmas Album	
	Worldwide 50 Gold Award Hits (Vol. 1)	
—	Almost in Love	DI
1971	That's the Way it is.	
	You'll never walk alone (Camden)	DI
—	Elvis Country (I'm 10000 years old)	
	C'Mon Everybody (Camden)	DI
—	Love Letters	DI
	The Other sides – Worldwide Gold Award	
	Hits (Vol. 2)	
	Wonderful World of Christmas	
	I Got Lucky (Camden)	
— 1972	"Elvis – Now!"	DI
—	He touched me	DI
—	Live at Madison Square Garden	
	Elvis Sings hits from his Movies	
	(Vol. 1). (Camden)	DI
	Burning Love and hits from his movies	
	(Vol. 2). (Camden)	
— 1973	Aloha From Hawaii Via Satellite	
—	Separate ways (Camden)	
	Elvis (Fool)	DI
1974	Having Fun on Stage with Elvis	DI
	Hits of the 70's	
—	Live on Stage in Memphis	
	A Legendary Performer	
—	Promised Land	
	Elvis' 40 Greatest (Arcade)	DD
—	Elvis' Christmas Album (Camden)	
1975	Elvis Today	
	Easy come, easy go (Camden)	
—	Elvis – US Male (Camden)	
	The Sun Collection (RCA Starcall)	
	Elvis Presley (Reader's Digest)	
— 1976	Pictures of Elvis (RCA Starcall)	

125

— Legendary Performer Vol 2
Elvis Presley Boulevard
The Elvis Collection (Camden)
— 1977 Elvis In Demand
— The Elvis Tapes (Redwood-Chiswick)
Welcome To My World
— MOODY BLUE
— ELVIS IN CONCERT

FOOTNOTE: Symbols used in this discography:

DD – Deleted Title, no longer available
II – Import Copies available (Record Deleted in UK)
DI – Deleted title in UK, import alternative available

For a complete catalogue of All British, USA, and European releases by Elvis Presley, send a stamped addressed envelope to:

ELVIS RECORD SERVICE,
41/43 Derby Road,
Heanor,
Derbyshire DE7 7QH,
England.

ACKNOWLEDGEMENTS

This work would not have been possible without the diligent research of 'super-fan' Miss Anne E. Nixon who lives in Stourbridge. Anne first became a fan in 1956, and since then has contributed more than 50 articles in *Elvis Monthly* including a 20,000 word part-work spanning Elvis' entire career. Her first contribution to the Elvis Fan Field was a drawing which was successfully published in the second issue of *Elvis Monthly*, back in 1960.

She has seen Elvis in concert in 15 performances at the Las Vegas Hilton, having travelled to the US on 5 separate occasions.

Anne's efforts have helped to form much of the backbone of this book, as too did the Jerry Hopkins' volume *Elvis*. Again, this biographer researched Presley's early career so well that any subsequent work cannot fail to draw comparisons. Any similarity therefore must be unavoidable.

Might I also thank Terry Mailey Jnr, and Miss Maria Davis for their research.

Bear with me whilst I conclude with a list of friends who through the years have supported my efforts: Jimmy Savile, OBE, Tom Lodge, Ian Bailye, Tony Prince, 'Rosko', Bob Bacon, Albert Hand (dec), Allen Harbinson (an illustrated biographer), Mark Wesley, David Wade (an unbeatable travel consultant), Keith Harris, Davy Jones, John Bogey, Hugh Downey (illuminated couriers), Alvin Stardust, Terry Loveland, Vic Porter, Ann Knight, Barbara Pendle, Ken Evans, Clifford Davis, Tony Atkinson, Bob Buffton, Alan Dykes and 'PK 521' – not forgetting Lizzie, Dawn, Jean and Arthur.

Warmest Best Wishes to Elvis & The Colonel.

TODD SLAUGHTER

THE AUTHOR

Todd Slaughter is 31 years old. Born in Leicester, England, he attended Alderman Newton Boys' School in the City. Upon leaving he worked for the Leicester Water Department, and then for a nationwide merchant of industrial pipeline equipment. When asked what he considers himself to be today, he replies 'an amateur entrepreneur'. Todd is married to a Scottish girl called 'Vikki', and they have a six-year-old son 'Gregory St John Slaughter'. 'We called him "Gregory St John", because we felt it would give him an advantage in later life should he want to become a television newscaster.' Todd has been secretary of Elvis' British Fan Club for over ten years.